S0-BZU-805

CANTERBURY STUDIES
IN ANGLICANISM
Apostolic Women, Apostolic Authority

CANTERBURY STUDIES
IN ANGLICANISM
Series Editors: Martyn Percy and Ian Markham

Apostolic Women, Apostolic Authority

Transfiguring Leadership in Today's Church

Edited by

Christina Rees and Martyn Percy
with Jenny Gaffin

Morehouse Publishing

CANTERBURY
PRESS
Norwich

Copyright © 2010 by The Contributors

First published in the United Kingdom in 2010 by the Canterbury Press Norwich
Editorial office
13–17 Long Lane, London, EC1A 9PN, UK
Canterbury Press is an imprint of Hymns Ancient and Modern Ltd
 (a registered charity)
St Mary's Works, St Mary's Plain, Norwich, NR3 3BH, UK
www.scm-canterburypress.co.uk

First published in North America in 2011 by
Morehouse Publishing, 4775 Linglestown Road, Harrisburg, PA 17112
Morehouse Publishing, 445 Fifth Avenue, New York, NY 10016
Morehouse Publishing is an imprint of Church Publishing Incorporated.
www.churchpublishing.org

Cover image, center, Baptism at Pentecost Festival, Boston Common, June 2000, courtesy of Episcopal Diocese of Massachusetts/David Zadig.

Cover image, bottom row, center, copyright © Kunstateliers Slabbinck nv.

Library of Congress Cataloging-in-Publication Data

Apostolic women, apostolic authority : transfiguring leadership in today's church / edited by Christina Rees and Martyn Percy ; with Jenny Gaffin.
      p.   cm. — (Canterbury studies in Anglicanism)
   "First published in 2010 by the Canterbury Press Norwich."
   Includes bibliographical references and index.
   ISBN 978-0-8192-2450-7 (pbk. : alk. paper)
   1. Women clergy. 2. Christian leadership. 3. Women in the Anglican Communion. 4. Christian leadership—Anglican Communion. 5. Anglican Communion—Doctrines. I. Rees, Christina. II. Percy, Martyn. III. Gaffin, Jenny.
BV676.A66   2011
262'.143—dc22

                                   2010045346

Canterbury ISBN: 978-1-84825-040-6

Typeset by Manila Typesetting Company
Printed in the United States of America

BV
676
.A66
2011

CONTENTS

v

Part 2 Leadership and Ecclesiastical Authority

Part 3 Facing the Change

Part 4 The Character of the Future

FOREWORD TO THE SERIES

by the Archbishop of Canterbury

The question 'What is the real identity of Anglicanism?' has become more pressing and more complex in the last decade or so than ever before, ecumenically as well as internally. Is the Anglican identity a matter of firm Reformed or Calvinist principle, resting its authoritative appeal on a conviction about the sovereignty and all-sufficiency of scripture interpreted literally? Is it a form of non-papal Catholicism, strongly focused on sacramental and ministerial continuity, valuing the heritage not only of primitive Christianity but also of medieval and even post-Reformation Catholic practice and devotion? Is it an essentially indeterminate Christian culture, particularly well-adapted to the diversity of national and local sympathies and habits? Is the whole idea of an 'ism' misplaced here?

Each of these models has its defenders across the Communion; and each has some pretty immediate consequences for the polity and politics of the global Anglican family. Some long for a much more elaborately confessional model than has generally been the case – the sort of model that those who defined the boundaries of the Church of England in the sixteenth century were very wary of. Some are happy with the idea of the Communion becoming a federation of local bodies with perhaps, in the long run, quite markedly diverging theologies and disciplines. The disagreements over the ordination of women and the Church's response to lesbian and gay people have raised basic issues around the liberty of local churches to decide what are thought by many to be secondary matters; the problem then being that not everyone agrees that they are secondary. The question of identity is inseparable from the question of unity: to recognize another community as essentially the same, whatever divergences there may be in language and practice, is necessary for any unity that is more than formal – for a unity that issues in vigorous evangelism and consistent 'diaconal' service to the world.

And this means in turn that questions about Anglican identity will inevitably become questions about the very nature of the Church – and thus the nature of revelation and incarnation and the character of God's activity. I believe it is generally a piece of deplorably overheated rhetoric to describe those holding different views around the kind of questions I have mentioned as being adherents of 'different religions'; but there is an uncomfortable sense in which this exaggeration reminds us that the line between primary and secondary issues is not self-evidently clear – or at least that what we say about apparently secondary matters may reveal something about our primary commitments.

The long and short of it is that we should be cautious of saying of this or that development or practice, 'It isn't Anglican', as if that settled the matter. One of the first tasks we need to pursue in the current climate is simply to look at what Anglicans say and do. We need to watch Anglicans worshipping, constructing patterns for decision-making and administration, arguing over a variety of moral issues (not only sexuality), engaging in spiritual direction and the practices of private prayer. Without this, we shan't be in a good position to assess whether it's the same religion; and we are very likely to be assuming that what we take for granted is the norm for a whole church or family of churches.

The books in this series are attempts to do some of this 'watching' – not approaching the question of identity in the abstract but trying to discern how Anglicans identify themselves in their actual life together, locally and globally. I'd like to think that they might challenge some of the more unhelpful clichés that can be thrown around in debate, the stereotypes used by both Global

South and Global North about each other. If it is true that – as I have sometimes argued in other places – true interfaith dialogue only begins as you watch the other when their faces are turned to God, this must be true a fortiori in the Christian context. And I hope that some of these essays will allow a bit of that sort of watching. If they do, they will have helped us turn away from the lethal temptation to talk always about others when our backs are turned to them (and to God).

We all know that simply mapping the plurality of what Anglicans do is not going to answer the basic question, of course. But it is a necessary discipline for our spiritual health. It is in the light of this that we can begin to think through the broader theological issues. Let's say for argument's sake that church communities in diverse contexts with diverse convictions about some of the major issues of the day do as a matter of bare fact manage to acknowledge each other as Anglican disciples of Jesus Christ to the extent that they are able to share some resources in theological training and diaconal service: the task then is to try and tease out what – as a matter of bare fact – makes them recognizable to each other. Not yet quite theology, but a move towards it, and above all a move away from mythologies and projections.

If I had to sum up some of my own convictions about Anglican identity, I should, I think, have to begin with the fact that, at the beginning of the English Reformation, there was a widespread agreement that Catholic unity was secured not by any external structures alone but by the faithful ministration of Word and Sacrament – 'faithful' in the sense of unadulterated by medieval agendas about supernatural priestly power or by the freedom of a hierarchical Church to add new doctrinal refinements to the deposit of faith. Yet as this evolved a little further, the Reformers in Britain turned away from a second-generation Calvinism which would have alarmed Calvin himself and which argued for a wholly literal application of biblical law to the present times and the exclusion from church practice of anything not contained in the plain words of scripture. Gradually the significance of a continuous ministry in the historic style came more into focus as a vehicle of mutual recognition, eventually becoming the straightforward appeal to apostolic episcopal succession often thought to be a central characteristic of the Anglican tradition.

The blend of concern for ordered ministry (and thus ordered worship), freedom from an uncritical affirmation of hierarchical ecclesiastical authority, with the appeal to scripture at the heart of this, and the rooted belief that the forms of common worship were the most important clues about what was held to be recognizably orthodox teaching – this blend or fusion came to define the Anglican ethos in a growing diversity of cultural contexts. Catholic, yes, in the sense of seeing the Church today as responsible to its history and to the gifts of God in the past, even those gifts given to people who have to be seen as in some ways in error. Reformed, yes, in the sense that the principle remains of subjecting the state of the Church at any given moment to the judgement of scripture – though not necessarily therefore imagining that scripture alone offers the answer to every contemporary question. And running through the treatment of these issues, a further assumption that renewal in Christ does not abolish but fulfils the long-frustrated capacities of human beings: that we are set free to sense and to think the texture of God's Wisdom in the whole of creation and at the same time to see how it is itself brought to fulfilment in the cross of Jesus.

This is the kind of definition that a sympathetic reading of the first two Anglican centuries might suggest. It certainly has implications for where we find the centre for such a definition in our own day. But the point is that it is a historical argument, not one from first principles; or rather, the principles emerge as the history is traced. Once again, it is about careful watching – not as an excuse for failing to look for a real theological centre but as a discipline of discerning the gifts that have actually been given to us as Anglicans.

Not many, I suspect, would seriously want to argue that the Anglican identity can be talked about without reference to Catholic creeds and ministry, or to think that a 'family' of churches can be spoken of without spelling out at least the essential family resemblances in terms of what Christ has uniquely done and what Christ continues to do in his Body through Word and Sacrament.

But to understand how this does and does not, can and cannot, work, we need the kind of exact and imaginative study that this series offers us. I hope that many readers will take the trouble to work with the grain of such investigations, so that our life in the Communion (and in communion itself in its fullest sense, the communion of the Holy Spirit) will be enriched as well as calmed, and challenged as well as reinforced.

+*Rowan Cantuar*
Lambeth Palace

FOREWORD TO THE U.S. EDITION

by Barbara C. Harris

Apostolic Women, Apostolic Authority: Transfiguring Leadership in Today's Church grows out of the volume *Transfiguring Leadership: Women in Today's Church*, the third book in the Canterbury Studies in Anglicanism series, a joint venture between Church Publishing Inc. in New York and SCM-Canterbury Press in London. In this volume, readers will be grateful for the opportunity to thoughtfully engage the topic of women in senior leadership in church and society, not only in the United States, but in various cultures across the globe. Resistance to women's leadership is not a phenomenon only in far off places, but has some residual and continuing persistence here at home. We need to pay continued attention to these important issues in light of urgent needs for authentic leadership in this second decade of the new millennium.

As the Church of England painstakingly inches its way toward welcoming women into the episcopate and increased numbers of other senior positions, and with some 21 years of female bishops in the United States and some fewer years in other Provinces of the Anglican Communion—including New Zealand, Canada and Australia—the whole question of women in authority—particularly ecclesial authority—commands more discussion. The preface to the UK volume thoughtfully raises the question: what do women distinctively bring to episcopacy as bishops, deans, archdeacons and in other forms of leadership that involve oversight?

I have addressed this question before and must return to one fact: we need women bishops for the same reason we need women priests—to complete that order of ordained ministry.* To look at the issue at a deeper level, we need to consider what women have brought to the office that enhances episcopacy and strengthens the church. A partial answer to that query may be found in the fact that many women tend to hold a sense of shared leadership and a collaborative management style, as opposed to the oft-times autocratic manner exercised by some males in authority. This mode of leadership, not exclusively feminine, has been likened to the reported business practice in Japan where a CEO often will consult on a new idea or an innovation with people at all levels of the organization, including the janitor, before instituting a new procedure. While the ultimate decision may still be made at the top of the corporate structure, it takes into consideration the ideas and concerns of those who must implement its components and must live with its consequences.

In some sense, many women in the church are more prone to living into a "movement psychology" as opposed to "an institutional modality." This means only that, in a movement, those who take the risks and do the work make the decision about what they will do. Institutions, on the other hand, are organizational entities where one group of people makes decisions regarding what another group of people will do. In the church, the former tends to recapture the sense of being part of Jesus' movement, while the latter, for many, seems to seek to make Jesus over into its own image.

That is my own observation, after several decades of serving the church and observing others in church leadership. The authors of this volume offer many more perspectives. Devoid of shrill rant and polemic, these essays offer reasoned and persuasive argument in the affirmative—women do bring special contribu-

---

*In *The Call for Women Bishops*, edited by Harriet Harris and Jane Shaw (Kelowna, BC: Wood Lake Books, 2005).

tions to ministries of oversight—and the contributors write out of shared experience of the church, both positive and negative, as well as the realities of our time. *Apostolic Women, Apostolic Authority* explores the scriptural, theological and ecclesiastical warrant for the election and appointment of women to positions of oversight. Facing into changes for the future, the contributors also examine the theology and distinctiveness of women exercising oversight and identify qualities, skills, experience and training needed to equip women for leadership positions.

Read this volume and consider that, even as numbers of women in ecclesiastical authority continue to increase, gross inequities are rampant. In the US, it has been reported that women earn about $10,000 less per year than their male counterparts and are mostly not found as rectors of cardinal parishes or deans of cathedrals.** In the UK and in the US, many women are non-stipendary or part-time and are mostly found in smaller churches or in ministry roles that do not include oversight of congregations or staff.

To many, the information contained herein may be new. To others, more accustomed to women in church leadership, it is probably old news. And yet, as women in secular careers and government continue to break through the "glass ceiling," one is left to wonder how long the "crystal dome" will remain unpierced in so many Provinces of the Anglican Communion. This is the time to read and hear the case for "transfigured leadership"—a call for Apostolic Women who, in Apostolic Succession, will exercise Apostolic Authority in God's Church and whose call by God to do so in the days ahead will become more wide-spread and more impossible to ignore or deny.

The Rt. Reverend Barbara Harris
Bishop Suffragan (retired),
The Episcopal Diocese of Massachusetts
October 2010

**Matthew Price, *The State of the Clergy Report* (New York: Church Pension Group, 2007), p. 10. See Appendix 1 in this volume for a summary of report findings.

ACKNOWLEDGEMENTS

This book grew out of an extraordinary gathering at Ripon College Cuddesdon in the run-up to the Lambeth Conference in 2008: the Transfiguring Episcope Conference to which one hundred women in positions of leadership around the Anglican Communion were invited.

There are many people to thank – both in relation to the conference, and to this book. First, special thanks are due to the entire staff team at Ripon College Cuddesdon for the planning and the hosting of the conference, and especially to Sophie Farrant for her facilitation of the event. And to all the volunteers who made it possible, including Julia Baldwin, Hannah Cleugh, Allie Kerr, Helen Rengert, Rosie Woodall, and many others. Second, to our Steering Committee who shaped the conference: Clare Amos, Faith Claringbull, Paula Gooder, Judith Maltby, Rosalind Paul and Flora Winfield, with additional input from Vivienne Faull, June Osborne, Jane Shaw and Sheila Watson. Christina Rees and Martyn Percy co-chaired the group. Third, to the very generous individuals and institutions that supported the conference, enabling all one hundred participants to attend on full bursaries, and especially Virginia Theological Seminary, St Andrew's Trust, The Foundation for Church Leadership, the Revd Robert Parker (a Governor of Ripon College Cuddesdon) and the Community of the Sisters of the Church. Fourth, to the Revd Dr Jenny Gaffin for all her help in the preparation of this text. Fifth, and finally, to all our authors – not all of whom were able to attend the conference – but have nonetheless helped share and shape our vision and hopes for transfiguring leadership in the Church today.

Martyn Percy and Christina Rees

ABOUT THE CONTRIBUTORS

Clare Amos is Director for Theological Studies in the office of the worldwide Anglican Communion. She has particular responsibility for work in the areas of theological education and interfaith concerns. Clare studied theology at Cambridge University then did postgraduate work in biblical studies at the École Biblique Jerusalem. She has taught biblical studies in Jerusalem, Beirut, Cambridge, London and Kent.

The Revd Canon Rosalind Brown is Residentiary Canon at Durham Cathedral, where she has responsibility for its nave, or public, ministry. The author of books on ministry and of many hymns, she was a town planner prior to ordination and also lived for a few years in the USA.

Sr Anita Cook is a member of the Community of the Sisters of the Church, which she joined in 1967. She has recently completed 11 years as the International Leader and UK Provincial, after serving as Provincial in Canada. She was ordained as a priest in 2007.

The Revd Dr Jenny Gaffin is Assistant Curate at St Peter's Parkstone, Poole. Prior to training for ordination at Ripon College Cuddesdon, she was a lay worker in London for almost seven years, working particularly with homeless people and in Soho's gay community. She holds a doctorate in lesbian and gay interfaith dialogue.

The Revd Lis Goddard is Chair of AWESOME, a group for evangelical ordained women in the Church of England. Since ordination she has worked as Chaplain of Jesus College, Oxford, a tutor at Wycliffe Hall, Oxford, assistant minister of St Andrew's, North Oxford, and associate vicar of St Mary's, Stoke Bishop.

The Revd Dr Helen-Ann Hartley is Tutor in New Testament at Ripon College Cuddesdon and holds a research fellowship at Harris Manchester College, Oxford. She is also Associate Priest in the Parish of Littlemore, Oxford. She studied theology at the University of St Andrews, Princeton Theological Seminary and Oxford. She is a member of the Commission for Theological Education in the Anglican Communion.

The Revd Dr Jane Hedges has been a Canon of Westminster Abbey for the past four years and has oversight for the ministry of welcome and hospitality to over a million visitors a year. Previously she has served as a team rector, canon pastor, stewardship adviser and team vicar. She is married with two teenage sons.

The Revd Dr Elizabeth A. Hoare is Tutor in Prayer, Spirituality and Mission at Wycliffe Hall, Oxford. Her interest in spirituality leans towards its historical aspects. She was ordained deacon in 1987 and was among the first women to be priested at Durham in 1994. Early on she felt drawn to the ministry of spiritual direction and it has remained a constant in her life.

Mrs Elizabeth Loweth is the Provincial Link for Canada to the International Anglican Women's Network, an official network of the Anglican Consultative Council. She has served as Human Rights Officer for the national programme of the United Church of Canada, and worked for interdenominational coalitions on Native Land Rights, the Immigration Act and World Population.

The Revd Canon Dr Charlotte Methuen is Lecturer for Church History and Liturgy at Ripon College Cuddesdon and University

Research Lecturer in Ecclesiastical History at the University of Oxford. She has taught at the universities of Hamburg and Bochum, and served as Diocesan Director of Training in the Diocese in Europe. She is Canon Theologian of the Cathedral and Diocese of Gloucester and currently assists in the Old Catholic parish of Bottrop, Germany. She has written extensively on the Reformation, ecumenism, and on the history of women's ministry.

The Revd Emma Percy is Chaplain and Welfare Dean, Trinity College, Oxford. She was ordained deacon in 1990 and priest in 1994. She has worked in parish and university posts, spending seven years as Vicar of Holy Trinity Millhouses, Sheffield. She is the Chaplain of Trinity College, Oxford. Married to Martyn Percy, she is the mother of two teenage boys and is currently working towards a PhD through Nottingham University.

Revd Canon Professor Martyn Percy is Principal of Ripon College Cuddesdon and the Oxford Ministry Course. He is also Honorary Professor of Theological Education at King's College London, Canon Theologian of Sheffield Cathedral, and an Honorary Canon of Salisbury Cathedral.

Christina Rees is a writer and religious commentator and a theologian working in the area of women and religion and contemporary Christian spirituality. She recently stepped down as Chair of WATCH (Women and the Church), a position she held for 13 years, and is a member of the General Synod and the Archbishops' Council. She is also a communications and media consultant and is the author of several books, including *The Divine Embrace* (HarperCollins, 2000, revised for DLT, 2006).

The Revd Kirsten Rosslyn-Smith is coming to the end of her curacy at St James', Tunbridge Wells. She is an artist and mother of three. Her husband Piers is thankfully an able family juggler and is at present a 'Dad at home'.

The Right Revd Catherine S. Roskam has been Suffragan Bishop of the Diocese of New York since 1996. She is engaged in ministry with congregations at home and, in concert with Anglican partners, in mission efforts around the globe, particularly, although not only, with regard to women and children.

The Most Revd Katharine Jefferts Schori was elected Presiding Bishop of the Episcopal Church in the USA in June 2006. She serves as Chief Pastor and Primate to the Episcopal Church's members in 16 countries and 110 dioceses. She joins with other principal bishops of the 38 member provinces of the worldwide Anglican Communion, seeking to make common cause for global good and reconciliation.

The Revd Canon Dr Jane Shaw was appointed as the new Dean of Grace Cathedral in San Francisco in June 2010. She was Dean of Divinity, Chaplain and Fellow of New College, Oxford, and Reader in Church History in the University of Oxford. She is also Canon Theologian at Salisbury Cathedral, and an Honorary Canon of Christ Church Cathedral, Oxford. She is the author of *Miracles in Enlightenment England* (Yale, 2006) and co-editor of *The Call for Women Bishops* (SPCK, 2004).

Canon Jane Steen is Chancellor of Southwark Cathedral and Director of Ministerial Education in the Diocese of Southwark. She developed an interest in leadership when reading Visitation Sermons for her PhD and subsequently serving as the Bishop of Southwark's Chaplain. She has been Canon Chancellor of Southwark Cathedral since 2005 and is responsible for diocesan continued ministerial education. She has particular concern for the newly ordained.

The Ven. Dr Joy Tetley, lately Archdeacon of Worcester, has been involved for many years in both ministry and theological education. She specializes in New Testament studies and ministerial theology, and has long had a passion for the Epistle to the Hebrews and its continuing significance. She is now based in

Oxford, engaged in a ministry of prayer, writing and counsel.

The Revd Rosie Ward is a leadership development adviser at the Church Pastoral Aid Society, where part of her role is to encourage and equip women as leaders in the Church. She previously served in three parishes in Bristol diocese, having been ordained in 1994. She has written several booklets and books, the most recent being *Growing Women Leaders* (BRF, 2008).

PREFACE

Rather like *Christ and Culture*, the first of the books in this *Canterbury Studies in Anglicanism* series, the inspiration for this volume came from the Lambeth Conference. Or, more accurately, from the prospect of the gathering in 2008 taking place, and recognizing that there would be entirely new dynamics involved. The realization that there would be at least a dozen women bishops attending prompted us to ask, 'What do women distinctively bring to episcopacy?' – as bishops, deans, archdeacons and in other forms of leadership that involve significant oversight.

Out of a number of meetings and conversations, a conference was born, which ultimately bore fruit at Ripon College Cuddesdon in 2008, in the days leading up to the Lambeth Conference. One hundred of the most senior Anglican women in the world gathered at Cuddesdon, to celebrate the ordained ministry of women and to explore the theology, ecclesiology and distinctiveness of women exercising oversight. It was a unique occasion; and, for many, something of an epiphany. We set ourselves an ambitious aim:

> The purpose of the conference is to explore new models of episcope and to reflect on the distinctive challenges facing women in positions of leadership in the Church. We will address issues such as power and authority, vocation and ambition, spirituality and theological formation in the context of exercising oversight within the Anglican Communion. We hope to identify the qualities, skills, experience and training needed to equip women in leadership.

We will examine what effective leadership might look like in its threefold context of the *diakonia*, priesthood and episcopate. We look forward to gaining different understandings and perspectives of leadership from around the Communion, and to identifying emerging theologies of episcope.

The conference will combine sessions with brief presentations from speakers followed by group discussion, Bible studies and times of worship. We will also be accompanied by a musician in residence and a theological reflector.

Those invited include all female Anglican bishops, other women in leadership in the Anglican Communion and senior women in the Church of England. A small number of men who are involved with identifying, supporting and promoting women in leadership are also invited. Together, our aim is to discover new ways of seeing how oversight may be exercised by the whole people of God.

The chapters in this book reflect several aspects of the extraordinary gathering that took place. Clare Amos begins our reflections with an introductory meditation on the meaning of transfiguration for leadership, using the transfiguration narratives to reflect upon women's leadership.

Part 1, on scripture and tradition, looks at women's leadership as it is represented in scripture and the traditional structures of the church. Helen-Ann Hartley, 'Follow Who? A Search for the Sacred Feminine in the New Testament', explores the identity and representation of women in the Bible. She then explores the implications of biblical themes of incarnation and creation on women's leadership in the contemporary Church. Rosie Ward, 'How did Jesus Develop Women as Leaders?', examines the question of discipleship and the ways in which Jesus himself nurtured the women who followed him. Charlotte Methuen, 'More Spirited than Lions': Apostolic Women and the Proclamation of the Gospel', continues the analysis of women's leadership, looking beyond the pages of the Bible and into the medieval period to uncover strong women's leadership in the early church. Sr Anita Cook CSC, 'Some Reflections on Women and Leadership in

Anglican Religious Communities', explores women's leadership in the context of Anglican religious communities. She argues for the place of 'followership' in the building and sustaining of life within the worldwide Anglican Communion.

Part 2, on leadership and ecclesiastical authority, examines the role that women leaders play within modern church structures. Cathy Roskam, 'Reflections on Women, Authority and the Church from an American Perspective', reflects on her journey to becoming a bishop in the Episcopal Church, and describes the changes she has seen as a result of the introduction of women bishops. She concludes with some thoughts on the way forward for women in the church. Jane Hedges, 'Women in Leadership', also offers some autobiographical reflections on her journey to becoming a Canon of Westminster Abbey. She presents the findings of some research she has undertaken into the experience of women in senior positions in the Church of England. Kirsten Rosslyn-Smith, 'Size Matters: Why Don't Women Lead Large Churches?', draws on the results of a survey of Rochester diocese in order to shed light on why women don't tend to lead large churches. She suggests reasons ranging from the demands of family, to the expectations of congregations, to theology. Jane Shaw, 'Women and Leadership: What's the Difference?', argues that in order to transform leadership, more is needed than simply the inclusion of people who are marginalized within existing structures. She argues for deeper institutional changes to free people to serve according to their gifts.

The chapters in Part 3, on facing change, explore from very different angles the nature and the challenge of the change that women bring about as they take on leadership roles in the church. Rosalind Brown, 'Benedict Revisited', examines what the Benedictine heritage has to teach us about how to go about engaging with the uncertainty and disorientation brought about by rapid changes to our collective religious life. Jenny Gaffin, 'In Search of a Spirituality of Authority', draws on experience of working in Soho's lesbian and gay community to reflect on how deeply enriching it can be to engage deeply with people who have been marginalized by the church. Joy Tetley, 'For God's Sake', roots the transitions and debates of the present time in the mystery of God's identity and relationship with humankind. She argues that the difficulties of the present time are all part of a journey towards a deeper, joyful relationship with God. Elizabeth Hoare, 'Evangelical Women, Spirituality and Leadership', explores women's leadership in the context of evangelical spirituality. She examines some of the obstacles to the growth of women's leadership in the evangelical strand of the tradition, and argues the case for change.

Part 4 looks ahead, imagining the future character of the church as women take on ever more senior roles. Emma Percy, 'What Clergy Do, Especially When it Looks Like Nothing', relates the task of parish ministry to the work of mothering. She argues that enabling clergy to find a language with which to talk about what they do will enable those exercising episcopal ministry to do so far more effectively. Elizabeth Loweth, 'Women, the Church and the World', presents an impassioned case for engaging with working to end violence and oppression against women around the world. She writes in the hope that as women come into powerful leadership roles within the church, they will be in a position to speak out against global injustices. Jane Steen, 'Episcope and Eiscope', examines the character of episcope, arguing that it is the quality of insight, rather than externals of gender, that identify a bishop. Lis Goddard, 'The Evangelical Burden and Imperative', shows the huge potential gift of evangelicalism in embracing women's leadership and shaping the future of the church. She outlines how existing models of episcopal authority might change for the better when women become bishops. The book concludes with Katharine Jefferts Schori's sermon at the closing Eucharist of Transfiguring Episcope, at All Saints' Parish Church, Cuddesdon, on 11 July 2008.

In bringing this conference together, the steering group were profoundly conscious of the ongoing debate relating to women bishops in the Church of England, and indeed in other parts of the Communion. The debate already belongs to a long history of debate and decision – about women deacons and women priests, and the passing of the 1993 Episcopal Act of Synod which created

Provincial Episcopal Visitors, the so-called 'flying bishops'. It has not been easy. Campaigns, committees and a multiplicity of considerations have characterized a complex and testing time for this corner of the Anglican Communion. Part of what the Transfiguring Episcope conference sought to achieve was not only to celebrate ordained women in roles of oversight, but also to examine their distinctive gifts and contributions that are being brought to our ecclesial polity and ordained ministries.

As important as it will be to have women as bishops, it is also important to see women in other positions of authority and leadership: according to a recent *Church Times* survey of almost 5,000 people, 80% have welcomed women priests, and 66% would welcome women bishops. True, the Church of England is not only a democratic body in which the will of the majority always prevails. But neither is it theocracy, governed by self-appointed guardians of the faith. The Church of England is a *via media*, part Catholic, part Reformed, part Episcopal and part Synodical.

The characters of these reflections – on the role of ordained women – take us to the heart of the dilemma for those who are charged with coming to a common mind about women bishops in the future. That heart is the identity of the Church, its theological methodologies and authorities. The identity of the Church is inherently contested, and the methodologies and authorities that it uses to clarify its life and define its identity are invariably incomplete and provisional. There can be no appeal to an absolute authority to decide a theological question. Theological questions can only be settled by ongoing theological work, earthed in the context of the contemporary church, and through a dynamic engagement with scripture, tradition and reason. We are continually reminded that attention to context is no less vital than to theological authority. Can we dare to trust that the Holy Spirit has gone on before us, speaking to the Church through culture and calling us to a more faithful embodiment of discipleship and to a new vision of unity and equality?

Our point about Anglican identity – and granted, much more could be said about this – may perhaps serve to remind us that the Church of England does not own the clear and settled ecclesiology that might be enjoyed by other denominations. There has always been room for the tradition of 'loyal dissent', and this now extends, arguably, to the Anglican Communion as a whole. Thus, Anglicans in the Diocese of Sydney can argue for (male) lay presidency at the Eucharist, and can trace their theological rationale not only in scripture, but also in tradition, by appealing to the seventeenth-century Puritan strain of Anglicanism that was once so influential. Thus, an apparently simple dispute about faith and order is not easily settled, since there is no one single tradition that makes up Anglicanism. As a Church it is inherently plural; a pottage of, at times, competing convictions held together by liturgical, familial, doctrinal, cultural, theological and other ties. It knows that compromise can be a virtue as well as a vice; for we have learned to value the complementarity and inherent challenge of a variety of distinctive traditions that on their own would be deficient. Disagreement can sharpen our thinking and bring rigour to our discussions on what it means to be faithful Anglicans.

Ultimately, the issue of women bishops cannot simply be settled by meta-theological arguments, and neither can it be done by epic or idealized accounts of the Church. We strongly suspect that having women as bishops will not pose quite the threat to unity that some suppose. There have been women bishops in the Anglican Communion for over 20 years, and currently women exercise episcopal ministry in four Anglican provinces, with a further 11 provinces having voted to have women as bishops. For the vast majority of members of the Church of England, women priests have been a welcome development. Since 1994 over 5,000 women have been ordained to the priesthood in the UK, now representing nearly 40% of all active serving Anglican clergy. As we go to press, the first draft of the women bishops legislation will be debated at General Synod and it is expected that the draft legislation will be sent out to the dioceses for further debate, before returning to General Synod for final approval.

When the Church accepts the ministry of women as bishops, it will be important to affirm the place of those who continue to engage in 'loyal dissent'. This is not meant to be patronizing; it will be a genuine confirmation of the Church's 'mixed pedigree' in regard to ecclesial polity. Those Anglo-Catholics and Evangelicals who cannot accept the mind of most in the Church will nevertheless be supported by the Church as a whole.

The long and historic debate about women bishops highlights the strengths and weaknesses of the Anglican Church, and its attempts to reach theological consensus on almost any matter. In a Church where compromise has often had to form the basis for communion, and where competing convictions have sometimes threatened to tear the Church apart, the debate offers a genuine opportunity to recover the *charity* as well as the *clarity* that we Anglicans need to live together as faithful disciples, yet also as those who do not always agree on matters of faith and order. A fuller appreciation and acceptance of the richness and variety of traditions that make up the Anglican Communion can help the Church to come to a deeper understanding of its precious (if sometimes precarious) polity. Consecrating women as bishops is, we believe, a necessary step for our established Church if we want to be taken seriously as a public and inclusive body. Consecrating women as bishops is also necessary if we are to realize the new vision of who we are as women and men who together make up the inclusive Body of Christ. We hope there will not be further delay. We also hope that not only those exercising episcope but all those in our Church will continue to be transformed by the unfolding revelation of the radiance of Jesus Christ.

Martyn Percy and Christina Rees

INTRODUCTION

Clare Amos

I enjoyed being part of the steering group for the Transfiguring Episcope conference. I have to confess, with a tweak of pride, that I am pleased to have made the original suggestion that we should make a link to 'transfiguration' – and then eventually to have suggested the title itself, Transfiguring Episcope.

The title has, of course, a double meaning, depending on whether episcope or, in its widest sense, pastoral leadership, is understood as the subject or the object of 'Transfiguring'. So this title both implies that through the development of the senior ministry of women we seek to transfigure the traditional nature and expectations relating to pastoral ministry – episcopal or otherwise – but also affirms that this ministry, properly exercised, 'transfigures' the life of the Church, and indeed the world.

Our excellent Bible studies, led by Paula Gooder, focused our attention on 2 Corinthians, chosen partly because it is the letter of Paul that explores the nature of ministry more extensively than any other. There is also that allusion to transfiguration in chapter 3, culminating powerfully with the words, 'And all of us, with unveiled faces, seeing the glory of the Lord as though reflected in a mirror, are being transformed [transfigured] into the same image from one degree of glory to another; for this comes from the Lord, the Spirit' (2 Cor. 3.18).

At the conference we didn't look in any detail at the transfiguration narratives in the Synoptic Gospels (Matt. 17.1–8; Mark 9.2–8; Luke 9.28–36) themselves, but in this Introduction I would like to explore these Gospel narratives, and use them as a resource and underpinning for my reflections.[1]

For a variety of reasons I have long been attracted to the theological motif of transfiguration, and believe that it is considerably undervalued in western Christianity. In eastern Christianity of course it is rather different, and the Feast of the Transfiguration is considered as one of the twelve great feasts of the Christian year. Having lived in the Middle East for ten years of my life, I grew to appreciate such Orthodox insights – reinforced for me by the fact that I relished the traditional site of the transfiguration on Mount Tabor. This is not necessarily where the transfiguration 'happened': indeed I am not sure exactly how helpful the category of 'happened' is in relation to the transfiguration. However, I stand in a long line of pilgrims who have felt that somehow on the top of Tabor the gap between heaven and earth manages (in spite of the tribulations of the modern Middle East which are apparent even on this mountaintop) to be 'tissue thin'.

Yet it is from a particularly Anglican viewpoint that my deepest appreciation of 'transfiguration' is found. Michael Ramsey, known for his own appreciation of the motif, famously summed up the glory of the transfiguration in words that cannot be bettered:

[The transfiguration] stands as a gateway to the saving events of the gospel, and is a mirror in which the Christian mystery is seen in its unity. Here we perceive that the living and the dead are one in Christ, that the old covenant and the new are inseparable, that the Cross and the glory are of one, that the age to come is already here, that our human nature has a destiny of glory, that in Christ the final word is uttered and in him alone the Father is well pleased. Here the diverse elements in the theology of the New Testament meet.[2]

What I find attractive about transfiguration from an Anglican perspective is the way that the motif holds together two different strands whose interweaving creates what is (in my view) the particular genius of Anglicanism: one strand being a reverence for tradition, dignity, worship and hierarchy, and the other which speaks of service, freedom, change and growth. The motif of transfiguration not only holds these two strands in a creative tension,[3] but works them together in such a way that each enriches the other. So what insights – with the help of the Gospel writers – can we draw from the transfiguration to inform our understanding of Anglican leadership?

Mark 9.2–8

We begin with Mark, not only because of Mark's likely place as the earliest of the Gospels, and the source for Matthew and Luke (at least in respect of the account of the transfiguration), but because of the key position the narrative of the transfiguration assumes in this Gospel. It is literally and structurally at the very centre of the Gospel. Although the story of the transfiguration is also important in Matthew and Luke, in neither Gospel does it form the 'heart' of the Gospel in quite the way it does in Mark. Mark's Gospel forms neatly into two halves. In the first half the challenge to the disciples, and to the readers, is that of Jesus' identity: 'Who do you say that I am?', answered by Peter's confession of faith at Caesarea Philippi (Mark 8.29), located almost immediately before the transfiguration. In the second half of the Gospel the question at issue is what does this identity mean for Jesus – and potentially at least for Jesus' first disciples and Mark's own readers. And it is the narrative of the transfiguration that draws the first thread to a climax, by its ratification of Jesus' identity; it also opens the pathway to the exploration of the vocation of suffering in the following chapters. From this mountaintop we can look both backwards and forwards, and see the whole in a clearer light. In this narrative of the transfiguration

3

Mark offers us a number of clues to help us make sense of his Gospel. Notice how the voice from heaven echoes the words spoken to Jesus at his baptism – but there is one significant difference. At the baptism (in Mark's Gospel) the voice speaks in the second person, apparently to Jesus alone, 'You are my beloved Son'; now the voice seems to address the inner core of the disciples who are present on this occasion, 'This is my beloved Son, listen to him.' In other words, at the transfiguration the meaning of Jesus' baptism seems to be expanded to include the nucleus of the Church – perhaps even the nucleus of a new humanity. Eastern Orthodox icons of the transfiguration traditionally show a circle of blue light or mandorla surrounding Jesus. This is intended to suggest that the meaning of the transfiguration is not complete until the entire world, the whole of creation, has been transfigured. So transfiguration invites us into a movement, a ripple effect, which begins with Jesus and invites us to share in the process. As we look upon the transfigured Christ we are being invited to be transfigured ourselves, so that the circle can extend further out. In the Old Testament there was a tradition that it was too dangerous to look on God. The transfiguration of Christ refines this tradition so that we discover that unless we are willing to be transfigured ourselves, that vision of the transfigured Christ is a vision too dangerous to behold.

However, the transfiguration points us not only to the beginning of Mark's Gospel but also to its end. The Italian architect Barluzzi, who built the church on the top of Tabor in the first part of the twentieth century, was aware of this. He was also responsible for the Church of All Nations in Gethsemane and he deliberately designed the two churches to provide a sharp contrast to each other, actually expressing in stone how the two narratives, of transfiguration and of agony in Gethsemane, interlock and help to interpret each other. The same three disciples are there on both occasions, but one is on the mountaintop and the other in a valley. One is an occasion suffused with light, the other a time of deep darkness, and Barluzzi captures this in his churches. At the transfiguration the voice from heaven calls Jesus 'my Son'. In Gethsemane Jesus prays to 'Abba', his Father. And the message of the heavenly voice to the disciples demanding obedience to the Son – 'Listen to him' – is curiously answered when Jesus in Gethsemane prays, 'My Father, not my will but yours be done.'

Constraints of space allow me to make only one further point about Mark's transfiguration narrative, and that is the interplay between life and death that suffuses the narrative. Prefacing the account of the transfiguration is Jesus' promise to his disciples that 'there are some standing here who will not taste death until they see that the kingdom of God has come with power' (Mark 9.1) – a promise of which in at least some sense the transfiguration is the fulfilment. At the conclusion of the narrative Jesus instructs the three who have witnessed it 'to tell no one about what they had seen until the Son of Man had risen from the dead' (Mark 9.9). The presence of Elijah with Moses – for that is the order in Mark – at the transfiguration may well be linked to the way that these two figures (and especially Elijah) were believed by Jewish tradition to have escaped normal human death. Though they float off the mountaintop at the end of the story, Jesus himself turns his face towards Jerusalem. Peter's wistful desire to build three 'dwellings' on the mountain surely resonates in some way with the pledge of Revelation that where God dwells with his people, death will be no more (Rev. 21.3–5). The power of the transfiguration story lies partly in the fact that it explodes a linear and chronological understanding of life and death: death – and resurrection – are to be found in the middle of life, not solely at the end of it.

So what lessons for transfiguring leadership does Mark's account of the transfiguration have for us?

The first is linked to the rippling circle. No matter where a bishop or priest is 'situated' within the scene of the transfiguration, whether 'identified' in some way with Jesus himself or set alongside the disciples, they are called by this story to be 'transfigured' themselves – not for their own glory but to facilitate the ongoing process of transfiguration of our world. The bishop who thinks that he or she has 'arrived' and can now therefore exist in a static state has failed in their vocation of transfiguring leadership. Additionally, as many in ministry would testify, it is often through our commitment to enable the others for whom we are pastorally responsible that we as pastors are ourselves transformed.

Another insight can come from reflecting on both Mark's narrative and the actual word *episcope*. Related to words for 'seeing', literally *epi-scope* means 'looking over', or 'overseer'. Part of the role of an overseer is perhaps to see all things in a synoptic whole, rather as Mark's transfiguration story gives us an oversight of his entire Gospel. To draw on Michael Ramsey's words about the transfiguration, we could suggest that it is the particular tasks of those called to episcopal ministry to see (and enable others to see) 'the Christian mystery . . . in its unity'. They need to honour the different aspects of this mystery, and those whose ministry and gifts mean that they emphasize one or other aspect, but their role is to hold together the whole and allow the different parts properly to inform each other. And as part of this 'seeing whole' is the need to give substance to the heart of the Christian mystery – that profound interplay between life and death to which Mark's transfiguration narrative witnesses.

Matthew 17.1–8

On the surface, Matthew's account of the transfiguration reads very similarly to that of Mark. There is, however, at least one difference – the note in verses 6–7 that the disciples who witness the event are overcome by fear and how in response Jesus touches them with the words, 'Do not be afraid'. Of course, it is famously typical of Matthew to 'heighten' experiences and emotions in this way, but in this instance the reassurance that Jesus offers also links to his care for the disciples, proto-representatives of the Church that is the object of Jesus' continuing care and concern. This is a key motif of Matthew's Gospel.

The other main alteration in Matthew's transfiguration account[4] is not obvious within the story itself. It is rather the place

6

of the story as a whole within Matthew's Gospel. The episode is not at the theological centre of the Gospel, as it is in Mark. That place is now probably accorded to Matthew's parable chapter, chapter 13. However, for Matthew mountains have a particular significance and his narrative of the transfiguration now forms part of a mountaintop sequence within the Gospel. So we have mountains of temptation (3.8); of preaching and teaching (5–7); of healing and feeding (15.29–39); of transfiguration (17.1–8); of the entry to Jerusalem (21.1); of eschatological prediction (24.3ff.) and finally of commissioning for mission (28.16–20). Although some of these mountains have parallels in Mark, several do not. What effect does setting the mountain of the transfiguration within this sequence create? All the mountains seem to allude to Sinai, and also hint at Jesus as one who is greater than Moses – having become the point where humanity and divinity intersect. But (at least by one reckoning) we can consider the transfiguration as the middle mountain of this list. More intensely than in any other of Jesus' experiences on a mountain it presents Jesus as the bridge between earth and heaven. The other mountains are all important for Jesus' busy ministry, for his feeding, healing and teaching of wounded humanity. Yet the placing of the transfiguration in the middle seems designed to remind us that such active ministries must be undergirded by a withdrawal in which the nature of reality can be – even if for only a moment – truly seen and become a source of refreshment.

So what does Matthew's transfiguration story have to say to us in relation to transfiguring leadership? Two observations. First, it speaks of the role of the pastor as one who stands before fellow disciples frightened and bewildered by what the twenty-first century has thrown at the Church: the leader who takes their hand and comforts them with the words, 'Do not be afraid'. For like Jesus himself, transfiguring leadership will seek to share the burden of the fear of others. Second, surely it is a reminder that it is the duty and the joy of all engaged in ministry, to seek times of withdrawal and prayer – time for the nurturing of the life of the Spirit.

7

Luke 9.28–36

Luke's account of the transfiguration is subtly different again. Notes that made their appearance in Matthew are now taken further in Luke. So, for example, although Matthew refers to the change in Jesus' face (17.2), in Luke's account the phrase 'the appearance of his face changed' (9.29) emphasizes this more strongly. Both Matthew (17.5) and Mark (9.7) refer to a cloud, but now Luke tells us that Jesus and the disciples actually entered this cloud. These changes help to emphasize the connection between the transfiguration of Jesus and Moses' experience at Sinai, as related in Exodus 24 and 33. This is further reinforced by the comment, only found in Luke, that Moses and Elijah conversed with Jesus about 'his departure [Greek, *exodus*] which he was about to accomplish at Jerusalem'. There is an intended allusion here to the biblical Exodus. Other differences include a reference to the fact that the disciples were weighed down with sleep, but had somehow managed to stay awake (9.32), that the event took place, typically for Luke, while Jesus was praying (9.29) and that after the experience the disciples kept silent (9.36).

What can we draw out of this for transfiguring leadership? I think that particular weight can be given to the way in which the Old Testament background is drawn on. Here, as elsewhere, Luke is telling us that moving forward in faith does not mean discarding the past, but revisiting it and seeing it in a new light. In Luke's theological schema we need to dig deep into the Old Testament to help us move forward, not only throughout Jesus' earthly ministry but also in the future life of the Church. Is not this a pattern for priestly ministry as well, certainly in its Anglican expression? One of the essential tasks for a priest in his or her role as 'guardian of the faith' is to be able to dig deep – and encourage others to do so – into the wells and resources offered by the Christian (and Jewish) past. But this is not to be merely an antiquarian exercise or a tenacious holding on to this past. Rather it is the sustaining of a dialectic between present and past that will enable new possibilities and a transforming future. And given the association of Exodus and liberation, that link to the

Exodus in Jesus' conversation with the prophets of old needs to be taken very seriously. It is interesting also to notice the link between prayer and the disciples' ability to stay awake (with the implication that if they had not done so they would have missed out on the experience of transfiguration). Surely both prayer and the ability to be 'on watch' are requirements for all in pastoral ministry – and the link between the two is equally important. It is also interesting to consider the disciples' silence about the event of transfiguration in the light of the famous remark of Ignatius of Antioch that bishops are most to be respected when they are silent. May there be an underlying connection between silence and transfiguration?

But there is one further point to note in relation to Luke and transfiguration. Just as Luke's Gospel reaches back into Old Testament roots, so also it encourages us to anticipate the life of the early church. And in the book of Acts, the Gospel's sequel, there is one person who is actually transfigured. It is rarely observed, but it is noted in Acts 6.15 that when he was on trial in front of the Sanhedrin, Stephen's face 'was like the face of an angel'. And though it is probably historically inaccurate to read the precise forms of later ecclesiastical ministries back into the pages of the New Testament, the ministry with which Stephen is normally identified is that of deacon. Can we draw out of this the implication that a bishop or priest, in order to be a vehicle of transfiguring leadership, must never forget that he or she also remains a deacon?

Final reflection

Given the context out of which the chapters in this book sprang, it is ironic to observe that none of the protagonists in the Gospel accounts of the transfiguration were female (unless one identifies the cloud in some way with the Shekinah!). Are women therefore excluded in some way from being part of the process of transfiguration? Perhaps the absence of women from this immediate Gospel episode should instead encourage us to ponder the ways in which transfiguration occurs – that it is not something that can be identified with or summed up in only one pinprick moment, but is an ongoing process. So, for example, can we talk about the 'transfiguration' that Jesus experienced through his discussion with the Syro-Phoenician woman who refused to take 'no' to her request to Jesus to heal her daughter? Or in John's Gospel, does not the dialogue between Jesus and the woman at the well of Samaria 'transfigure' them both? There are other examples one could give. But it is of interest to note that the word 'over-shadow' (*episkiazo*), which appears in Matthew's and Luke's transfiguration narratives to describe the cloud overshadowing Jesus and the disciples (Luke 9.34), occurs on only one other oc-casion in Luke's Gospel: in 1.35, when the angel tells Mary that the power of the Most High will 'overshadow' her, so that she will give birth to the holy child. An exploration of transfigura-tion in terms of pregnancy and birth-giving would be fascinating and would offer a potentially rich theological seam in which to quarry. What might that mean for 'transfiguring leadership?

PART I

SCRIPTURE AND TRADITION

I

FOLLOW WHO?

A Search for the Sacred Feminine in the New Testament

Helen-Ann Hartley

From the age of 11 up to 18, I was educated by the Sisters of Mercy at St Anthony's School in Sunderland, in the north-east of England. Alongside a regular diet of Bible study, I was exposed to the myriad prayers that cluster around the Virgin Mary, and at first I found it quite bewildering. Gradually, however, my understanding of the role that Mary played in the life and ministry of Jesus became part of my own general appreciation of the roles that women and men played in the pages of the New Testament. Above all, the stories in the New Testament point to the profound richness of human diversity. Indeed, human diversity is part of the extravagance of creation. As much as I find myself wanting to celebrate this extravagance, I am deeply troubled by the ways in which the texts of the Bible are misread and used to harm rather than to heal, to exclude rather than to include. In fact, the Bible does both (it promotes inclusion as well as exclusion), and this is part of the complexities in interpretation that are too often ironed out to create one perspective that sets the agenda for debate.

A story on the BBC News website, entitled 'Paradise lost', spoke about how satellite navigation devices are starting to erode local knowledge.[1] The article suggested that the increasing popularity of such devices is not just about the advance of

13

technology. It speaks to our contemporary anxieties and pre-occupations about the road. More roads and better cars mean that we can travel further, and so the risk of getting lost is all the greater. I wonder if that sense of anxiety can be applied to reading the Bible? The more ways we have of interpreting its texts, the less clear our path apparently becomes, and the greater the risk of getting lost on the way. It strikes me that the desire of some to return to a perceived 'orthodoxy' is symptomatic of a deep anxiety at the democratization of interpreting the Bible. The notion that all can join in, ask questions, and have a say in how the Bible is read is too dangerous for some.

In thinking about the feminine in the New Testament, this search for wholeness of humanity is very much to the fore. Women contribute to the biblical narrative as much as their male counterparts, only sometimes it is harder to hear their voices. But at this point it is important to assert that we are dealing with (by and large) first-century Mediterranean texts; and that we need always to remember that our texts tell us only part of the story! Moreover, as extensive research on aspects of the social setting of the New Testament has demonstrated, cultural dynamics such as honour and shame played a crucial role in determining the place of women, in ways that are more complex than in our own western society (or perhaps just different). An aspect of our ongoing task therefore has to be how to read texts that are from a time and culture very different from our own, and yet are the basis for profound change and challenge in our contemporary world. One of the first things that I always tell my students is that the word 'criticism' is not a negative. It is by asking critical questions that we ultimately grow; we may not always get the answers, but there is a lot to be said for pondering: asking, searching, seeking; and holding words like 'critical' and 'creative' in the same breath when we read the Bible.

So who are the women in the New Testament? How are they portrayed? What do they tell us, and what are the themes that emerge? Given that several passages in the New Testament are often used to suppress the role of women, how and where do potential role models emerge? Or indeed, do we need to look beyond just the characters, towards a radical re-presentation of the meaning of humanity and the role the incarnation plays in that? While much of the material that follows is not exactly new, it seems worthy of restating something of the presence of women in the New Testament, texts that are foundational in the search towards the wholeness of humanity.

Women in the ministry of Jesus

From just a cursory examination of the Gospels, it might be possible to see Jesus as just another advocate of a patriarchal society, since he chose twelve men to be his personal followers. This is only one side of the story, however, for the Gospels also portray Jesus as one who accepted women both as followers and as travelling companions:

> And the next thing was that he made his way through town and village proclaiming, and preaching the good news of the kingdom of God; and the Twelve [were] with him, and certain women, who had been cured from evil spirits and sickness, Mary called Magdalene, from whom seven demons had come out, and Joanna the wife of Chuza, Herod's stewards, and Susanne, and many other women, who ministered to them from their resources. (Luke 8.1–3)[2]

It seems, too, that Jesus rejected many levitical laws about being clean and unclean, since he apparently associated with the unclean, allowed unclean women to touch him, and was willing to touch a corpse and stop a funeral procession to help a woman (Mark 5.25–34 and parallels; Luke 7.11–17, 36–50).[3]

Further light is shed on Jesus' attitude towards women by the sayings that suggest that among his followers the family of faith becomes the primary group of identification:

> Do not think that I came to bring peace on earth: I didn't come to bring peace but a sword! I came to turn a man against his

father and a daughter against her mother and a bride against her mother-in-law; and a person's enemies are the people of his household. The one who loves father or mother more than me is not worthy of me. And anyone who does not take up their cross and follow after me is not worthy of me. The one who finds their life will lose it; and the one who loses their life for my sake will find it. (Matt. 10.34–39)

In Acts, Luke presents a woman as a prophetess (21.9); as a religious teacher of a notable male Christian leader (18.1–3, 24–26); as a hostess for a house church (12.12–17); the first convert in a new region (16.12–40); and as assuming the roles deaconesses were later to have (9.32–42). Luke mentions that church meetings took place in the homes of women (Acts 12.12; 16.40); and notes the presence of women at key points in the narrative of the spread of the Gospel: from Jerusalem (1.14; 12.12–17), to Joppa (9.36–42), to Philippi (16.11–15), to Corinth (18.1–3), to Ephesus (18.19–26), to Thessalonica (17.4), to Beroea (17.12), and to Athens (17.34).

In John, there are at least five episodes that feature women and their roles: Mary, Jesus' mother (chapters 2, 19); the Samaritan woman (chapter 4); Mary and Martha (11 – 12); the women at the cross (19); the appearance of Jesus to Mary Magdalene.

Taken together, these stories reveal women on their way to becoming Jesus' disciples, progressing in understanding and faith in Jesus. Particularly interesting and indeed radical is Jesus' encounter with the Samaritan woman at the well in John 4. She is presented as bringing the good news about Jesus to her neighbours in words they can understand; Jesus encounters her, steps back, and allows her to flourish. John 20 is very important too, for here we find not only that a woman received the first appearance of the risen Lord, but also that she was commissioned to be an evangelist to the eleven, proclaiming the good news to them (and in that sense it is possible to argue that theology and leadership both begin with proclamation of the resurrection):

16

Jesus says to her, 'Don't touch me – for I have not yet gone up to the Father. But go to my brethren and tell them, "I am going up to my Father and your Father, and my God and your God."' Mary the Magdalene comes announcing to the disciples, 'I have seen the Lord', and that he had said these things to her. (John 20.17–18)

The Apostle Paul: a'paul'ling or appealing?

O St Paul where is he that was called
the nurse of the faithful, caressing his sons?
Who is that affectionate mother who declares everywhere
that she is in labour for her sons?
Sweet nurse, sweet mother,
who are the sons you are in labour with, and nurse,
but those whom by teaching the faith of Christ
you bear and instruct?
Or who is a Christian after your teaching
who is not born into the faith and established in it by you?
And if in that blessed faith we are born
and nursed by other apostles also,
it is most of all by you,
for you have laboured and done more than them all in this;
so if they are our mothers, you are our greatest mother.[4]

If I were to begin an introductory class on the Apostle Paul by quoting this prayer of St Anselm, a not inconsiderable number of eyebrows would be raised. Paul is frequently portrayed as a misogynistic bigoted individual, intolerant of many and passionate about his own faith. But this is at best a caricature, at worst a gross insult to a complex person who was forced to piece together his identity after his vision of the risen Christ. It's true that Paul's letters contain some uncomfortable words about the role of women (as in fact they do about men), but as this prayer suggests, there's more to Paul than meets the eye.

When we investigate the letters of Paul, we find concepts already in evidence in the Jesus tradition. On the one hand, there is an affirmation of marriage and family (1 Cor. 7, which places an emphasis on equality quite radical for its context, one might argue; 1 Cor. 11, a passage not without difficulty of interpretation). On other hand, the family of faith is seen as the primary unit of identity and there is clear evidence of women assuming important roles in the Christian community, including that of proclamation, as Romans 16 makes clear:

> I commend to you our sister Phoebe, a deacon of the church at Cenchreae, so that you may welcome her in the Lord as is fitting for the saints, and help her in whatever she may require from you, for she has been a benefactor of many and of myself as well . . .

The fact that Paul is writing letters that are addressed to specific situations at a specific time must be taken into consideration when evaluating such difficult texts as:

> As in all churches of the saints, let wives refrain from speaking in the churches. For it is not permitted for them to speak; rather let them be subordinated, as the Torah says. If, however, they wish to learn something, let them enquire of their own husbands at home. For it is a disgrace for a woman to speak in the assembly . . . (1 Cor. 14.34–35)

and its parallel in 1 Timothy 2.8–15. Paul, and the Paulinist writer of 1 Timothy, are both dealing with problems in the communities. The rulings given apply to specific problems of women disrupting the worship service, or usurping authority over others. In both cases, the abuses are being ruled out, but this does not foreclose the issue of whether or not women who did not abuse their privileges might speak or exercise authority if it was done in a proper and orderly manner. In fact, in view of the evidence that various women were Paul's co-workers in the Gospel ministry it is unlikely that these texts were ever intended to do more than rule out certain abuses.

Aside from the specific citation of women's names and the odd text that creates difficulty of interpretation (wondering just what was going on in some of Paul's communities), one of the truly remarkable things about Paul is the way in which his tone often incorporates a distinctly feminine perspective (as St Anselm's prayer might suggest). This was initially brought to my attention some 14 years ago when I was a graduate student in the United States, by Beverly Gaventa, who has written extensively on the topic. She calls to attention passages such as these:

> But we became babes in your midst, as a nurse cherishes her own children. (1 Thess. 2.7)

> Brothers, I was not able to speak to you as to spiritual people but as to fleshy people, as to babes in Christ. I gave you milk to drink, not solid food, for you were not yet able, but even now you are not able. (1 Cor. 3.1–2)

> My children, with whom I am in labour again until Christ is formed in you . . . (Gal. 4.19)

And speaking about the 'end times':

> Then sudden destruction will come upon them as labour pangs upon a pregnant woman . . . (1 Thess. 5.3)

> For we know that all creation groans together and labours together even until now . . . (Rom. 8.22)[5]

Taken at face value, they do suggest that there is more to Paul than one first assumes, and we should not dismiss him as being 'anti-woman'. Indeed, it seems that in the early church, such maternal imagery was radically key to the reception of Paul's message. The second-century *Acts of Paul and Thecla* records Paul's execution. When struck by the executioner's sword, so the story goes, what Paul's body yielded up was not blood but milk. The narrator concludes: 'The soldier and all who stood by were amazed, and glorified God who had given Paul such glory.'

The 'sacred in the feminine' – incarnation and creation

In my everyday teaching I am engaged in the training and formation of women and men who are training for public ministry in the Church. However, theology is everybody's business; theology is not a luxury but rather is something that every person is involved in, whether we realize it or not. Change doesn't happen just because someone at the top says so; our collective task is to think about how everyone can speak into the body of Christ what God has given them to speak. This is in part what the gospel message is about, and is what the New Testament says to us about the roles of women (and others). What I am saying is that it is not enough simply to state what the stories about women in the New Testament are and leave it at that: the next step involves relating the contribution that these stories make to our overall understanding of the tasks of Christian discipleship today. The gospel is not about putting ourselves with people we are most like (tempting though that is), it is surely about putting ourselves with the people we are most *unlike*.

I want to suggest that one way of beginning to articulate the 'sacred in the feminine' is through reflecting on the themes of incarnation and creation, which when taken seriously articulate what this radical call to discipleship is about – partly because I want to tentatively suggest that both may be portrayed in very feminine terms (not solely feminine, but in a way that is more inclusive than exclusive and that challenges our perceptions of power dynamics and gender). Here let me briefly explain.

The story of the divine becoming human happens because a woman (Mary) says 'yes'. I personally don't have a great deal of time for the feminist argument that says that Mary didn't have a choice in the matter, because the Bible is full of stories of women and men who are given impossible tasks to fulfil, and according to the text, Mary joyfully responded to her task. However, it is a Pauline articulation of the incarnation that makes the point most clearly. In Paul's letter to the Philippians 2.5–8 he writes this:

> Let your thinking be what was in Christ Jesus, who, being in the form of God, did not think it plunder to hang on to (the being equal to God). Instead he emptied himself, taking a slave's form, coming to be in the likeness of human beings. And being found in appearance like a human being, he humbled himself! He became obedient even to the point of death (death on a cross!).

Power is about stooping down voluntarily so that we might all come up together. Our drive must be to search constantly for groups who are in the minority. Sadly the model of power that prevails in the world (and often the Church) is often grounded in the desire for prominence and the promotion of tribalism from which women are too often excluded. In many parts of the world women are denied access to theological education, to theological resources and to the potential to become theological educators in their own right. Alongside this is the theme of creation – in which, surely, women and men are invited together to play a full and equal part. If we aim to put the feminine back into the sacred, then surely the fullness of creation is articulated?

Any encounter with the texts of the Bible should leave us, women and men together, changed, but not always in the ways we might necessarily expect. For me this is perhaps best summed up in the words of John Newton (1725–1807):

> I am not what I ought to be,
> I am not what I want to be,
> I am not what I hope to be,
> But by the grace of God
> I am not what I was.

2

HOW DID JESUS DEVELOP WOMEN AS LEADERS?

Rosie Ward

In New Testament times the teacher/learner method of intentional discipling was a widely recognized method of teaching, and Jesus used it to train the future leaders of his church. In a growing body of literature on Christian leadership, it is common to read about how Jesus developed leaders, as a model for developing leaders today. For example, according to the model based on Mark 3.13–19, used in *Growing Leaders* by James Lawrence (and also used in the Church Pastoral Aid Society 'Growing Leaders' course),[1] Jesus chose the twelve disciples, appointed them to be with him, and appointed them to go out for him (a pattern that can be summed up with the three words *identify*; *invest*; *entrust*). Another model is based on Luke 5.1–11, where Jesus began to call his disciples and train them for future leadership.

But what of women? If in the early churches we see women emerging into leadership alongside men – women such as Lydia (Acts 16.14, 40), Euodia and Syntyche (Phil. 4.2–3), Phoebe (Rom. 16.1–2), Priscilla (Acts 18.18; Rom. 16.3–5; 2 Tim. 4.19), Junia, 'outstanding among the apostles' (Rom. 16.7), and Nympha (Col. 4.15), plus many others known from early church documents – is it possible to see how some women were identified, invested in and entrusted with leadership responsibility also? I believe it is. In the Gospels we can see how Jesus, while choosing twelve men as a primary group of disciples, also began to develop women, changing inherited patterns and beginning to restore to the Church and the world the partnership of men and women that was lost at the Fall.

The twelve and the women

Jesus appointed twelve men as his disciples. This is sometimes used as a reason why women should not be in particular forms of ministry and leadership, but it is more often seen as an inevitable concession to the culture of the day: the ministry of women apostles would have been unacceptable when the testimony of a woman was disregarded in a court of law. The choice of twelve men was also a symbolic act: twelve male apostles, corresponding to the twelve patriarchs and the twelve tribes, was an eschatological sign denoting that Jesus was reconstituting the ancient people of God.

However, while the twelve clearly have a special place, it is also clear that they were not intended to be unique in ministry, first because the nature of ministry had changed, and second because Jesus also chose and sent out others. Among this number and, like the twelve men, close to Jesus, were a number of women followers, whose pattern of discipleship and potential leadership closely mirrors that of the men. The fact that women were followers at all in a culture where few women were literate or had any formal education is in contrast to the accepted practices of the day (women were discouraged in rabbinic laws from leaving their homes). By highlighting findings from recent scholarship on the Gospels, it is possible to argue that Jesus developed women as leaders by encouraging them to follow him in preparation for when they in turn would lead others.

Luke 8.1–3 is one key passage. Here we see that a number of women accompanied Jesus, along with the twelve (who are listed in 6.12–19). In his study of named women in the Gospels, *Gospel Women*, Richard Bauckham cites a definition of this

23

'summary' statement: it indicates that the circumstances described happened 'repeatedly within an indefinite period of time'.[2] In other words, while this is one brief reference, it indicates that women regularly accompanied Jesus in this way.

Bauckham also challenges the NRSV translation, and argues that the Greek text makes it clear that both the twelve *and* the women 'were with' Jesus, rather than the women being something of an afterthought: he suggests that the text should read 'There were with him the twelve and some women who . . .'[3] Here Luke is singling out two groups among the larger body of disciples, the twelve and the women. The fact that the women provided for him is not the key point: the point is that they were 'with' Jesus. This is the essence of discipleship: to accompany Jesus and to witness his ministry, and both men and women seem to be seen as equals in discipleship. At this point in the Gospel narrative, neither men nor women are actively participating in Jesus' ministry, but both are being prepared to do so.

Throughout the Gospels there are two groups of disciples – those who left their homes and families literally to follow Jesus, and others who listened to Jesus as he came to them. Luke reminds his readers here that women were among those who literally followed Jesus as well as among those who flocked to hear his teaching. Bauckham makes it clear that these women were not being assigned a gender-specific role, such as women ordinarily played in a family situation. They must have been unusual women to have had independent means, and the text does not imply that none of the male disciples provided materially in this way, but only that a number of women did provide support for Jesus and his disciples. The twelve have made similar sacrifices in giving up home and family to follow Jesus (Luke 5.11). For aristocratic women such as Joanna it must also have been costly to follow, in that it would have appeared scandalous that women attached themselves to a group such as Jesus and his largely nonelite followers. Thus the discipleship of women is conceived as radically as for men – perhaps even more radically.

It is also interesting that there are differences between Luke and Mark/Matthew in the way discipleship is conceived: Luke characteristically envisages a larger group of disciples. While Luke also makes reference to 'the twelve', Bauckham notes that these are all in material that derives from Mark, with the exception of Luke 8.1–3 and two post-resurrection appearances.[4] As we read, for example, the story of the road to Emmaus and Jesus' appearance to Cleopas and another disciple (Luke 24.13, 18, 33, 36), we become aware that 'discipleship' is not confined to the twelve.

All the Synoptic Gospels speak of women accompanying Jesus in his travelling ministry (Matt. 27.55–56; Mark 15.40–41; Luke 23.49). They are there at the cross (Luke 23.27, 49) and the tomb (Luke 23.55), which must have taken some courage. They witnessed the resurrection (Luke 24.1–11). In John's Gospel, women are given places as exemplary disciples and fully fledged apostles, which some have argued is evidence for women's leadership in the Johannine community.[5] Mary Magdalene is the premier example.

In Luke 9 we read how the twelve are sent out; Jesus gave them 'power and authority to drive out all demons and to cure diseases, and he sent them out to proclaim the kingdom of God and to heal those who were ill' (9.1–2). This is one of relatively few occasions in the Gospels where we see the twelve actually involved in ministry (9.6). In chapter 10 we read how 72 others are sent out, and it seems highly likely that women are included among these, given the emphasis Luke places on the women who followed Jesus, and that there are hints in the New Testament of husband and wife missionary teams (Priscilla and Aquila, Andronicus and Junia in Rom. 16.3 and 7) and of pairs of women (Tryphena and Tryphosa in Rom. 16.12). Thus women, while not being chosen in the same way as the twelve, were certainly 'with' Jesus, invested in, and then entrusted with ministry.

Thus, some scholars suggest, the differences between the groups of men and of women followers of Jesus were not as great as might at first appear. The women were 'with' him throughout his ministry, observing him, and being prepared for the time when, after the resurrection, they in turn would be commissioned for ministry.

Women at the rabbi's feet

Jesus welcomed many different women as learners: Mary of Bethany, the woman at the well, the Canaanite woman, and others who are not named. Mary sat at Jesus' feet, which was the normal attitude of someone who was a disciple and who would subsequently be a teacher. Thus Jesus clearly affirms a woman's right to be a disciple and not to be solely concerned with what might be thought 'women's' domestic work. And Jesus rebukes her sister Martha for her failure to 'listen', in her anxiety to attend to the normal domestic duties that would be expected of women (Luke 10.41–2). While the contrast between Martha and Mary is sometimes used to explore active and reflective lifestyles, it is hard to find anything more counter-cultural than Mary's behaviour in terms of what women were expected to be and do.

John's account of the death of Lazarus (John 11.17–44) also repays close attention. The centre of the story is not Lazarus, but the conversations Jesus has with Martha and Mary, especially the former. Her confession of faith reveals that she has indeed learned at Jesus' feet, and she makes a clear declaration of faith (11.27), similar to that of Peter. Mary (11. 32) exhibits the same faith and forthrightness.

In John 12.1–8 we read how Mary anoints Jesus' feet – which interestingly anticipates the foot-washing in chapter 13. The interrelation between these two passages shows how Mary models service and discipleship, and participation in Jesus' suffering and death. In her study of gender in Luke–Acts, *The Double Message*, Turid Seim explores the pattern of servant leadership that Jesus modelled and taught. She notes that in Luke the women exhibit a Christ-like pattern of service, in contrast to the Pharisees and other groups of leaders (whom Jesus criticizes), and to those disciples who in their leadership seem motivated by a desire for position (Mark 9.34/Luke 9.46; Mark 10.35–37). Seim also suggests that Luke 8.1–3 is one place where this 'leadership is service' theme is summed up, and that the stress on women's servant leadership helps to redefine the function of leadership exercised by men, giving them an 'examplary significance'.[6]

Two other passages in Luke make it clear that discipleship (and potentially ministry) belongs to women as well as to men. On one occasion, when Jesus is told that his mother and brothers have come to see him, he replies: 'My mother and my brothers are those who hear God's word and put it into practice' (Luke 8.19–21). This is what Jesus encouraged Mary to do – to listen and to put into practice. A few chapters later, when a woman calls out to Jesus, 'Blessed is the mother who gave you birth and nursed you', Jesus replies: 'Blessed rather are those who hear the word of God and obey it' (11.27–28). This tells us, first, that there were women in the crowd, and also that, as Ruth Edwards puts it, 'Jesus was not prepared to affirm the primary role of biological motherhood, either for Mary, his own mother, or for any other woman.'[7] A woman is to be fulfilled not primarily through her role as a wife and mother, but through following Jesus. The blessing is for men *and women* who are obedient to God's will.

Apostle to the apostles

Finally, Jesus' appearance and commissioning of Mary Magdalene, after his resurrection, has been much discussed. Mary has suffered in popular thinking, through her confusion with other Marys and the mistaken assumption that she was a prostitute. But among the followers of Jesus, Mary's name occurs more often than most of the twelve apostles. Of the women who knew Jesus, only Mary his mother is mentioned more times than Mary Magdalene. All four Gospel writers identify her as one of Jesus' most devout followers, and she appears in nine different lists of women, in all but one with her name heading the list.

When Mary recognized the resurrected Jesus, she cried out, 'Rabbouni', which means 'my teacher' (John 20.16). This, and the fact that she was one of the women travelling with Jesus, and thus alongside him to learn, shows that she was indeed a disciple of Jesus, learning from him in order that she should in turn be a teacher and leader.

27

For the first disciples, being a follower of Jesus was much more than being the follower of any other rabbi. The future of the Christian faith depended on Jesus' students and how they succeeded in passing on what they learned from him, by teaching what he taught them and by loving one another as he loved them. It seems that women were included in this, and this can hardly have been unintentional on Jesus' part when for him to associate with women at all, let alone allow them in his travelling group, would have invited adverse comment.

The high point of the story has to be in the garden, where Jesus commissions Mary with the task of telling the good news of the resurrection to his brothers, the eleven apostles. No wonder she has been called the 'apostle to the apostles',[8] and if the qualification of an apostle is to have been with Jesus and witnessed the resurrection, then she (and other women) qualified, even if their position was not formalized in the process of replacing Judas (Acts 2.21–22).

Having seen such a high-profile woman in the Gospels, it is somewhat frustrating that we do not see her again in the rest of the New Testament – hence, perhaps, the amount of speculation there has been about her story. But we may gain further insight into Mary as a leader in the *Gospel of Mary*, a piece of writing that came to light around the turn of the twentieth century. While we cannot give it the same status as the canonical Gospels, it does point to Mary having a clear leadership role in the early Church. This leadership was, however, disputed by some of the other disciples, primarily Andrew and Peter, the latter opposing her ministry partly because 'her leadership lowers his gender status'.[9] Thankfully, modern scholarship (as opposed to sensationalism) has recaptured the New Testament picture of Mary Magdalene as prominent disciple, which was so long eclipsed by Mary Magdalene the reformed prostitute.

Carolyn Custis James suggests that culturally it would have been acceptable for the apostles to marginalize the female followers of Jesus after he returned to the Father.[10] But it was not acceptable to Jesus. He had elevated women by including them as disciples and at his resurrection he affirmed their ministry as

28

messengers. The Gospel writers were dependent on the testimony of women such as Mary his mother as well as Mary Magdalene for reconstructing the narrative of Jesus' life, death and resurrection. Mary his mother, and 'the women' were there after the resurrection, devoted to prayer and waiting for the future to unfold (Acts 1.14). And when the Spirit was poured out at Pentecost, everything changed. The prophecy of Joel, that God would pour out his Spirit on *all* his people, was fulfilled:

> Your sons and your daughters will prophesy,
> Your young men will see visions,
> Your old men will dream dreams,
> Even on my servants, both men and women,
> I will pour out my Spirit in those days, and they will prophesy.
> (Acts 2.17–18)

Women as well as men were equipped by God's Spirit for all that he would call them to do.

From these examples, we can see that Jesus inaugurated a new way, a new attitude to women, recognizing that what mattered was their response to God rather than the roles that society dictated for them. As he invested in the twelve male disciples, so he also invested in those women who chose to follow him throughout his ministry. And when the Spirit was poured out at Pentecost, God's new society was established, and women as well as men were empowered. We are now more aware than we used to be of the cultural background in which the early Church came to birth, where in Greek and Roman society women were used to having a role in religious leadership, so that in some contexts it was not so hard for women to step into leadership in churches as they were being established in homes, and for their leadership to be accepted. In the first churches, old distinctions of race, class and gender were abolished; qualification for service depended (with a few cultural concessions) no longer on gender and societal position but on gifting, and those women who had been 'with' Jesus were able, until restrictions were made,[11] to serve alongside men.

29

3
'MORE SPIRITED THAN LIONS'

Apostolic Women and the Proclamation of the Gospel

Charlotte Methuen

Then Jesus summoned his twelve disciples and gave them authority over unclean spirits, to cast them out, and to cure every disease and every sickness. These are the names of the twelve apostles: first, Simon, also known as Peter, and his brother Andrew; James son of Zebedee, and his brother John; Philip and Bartholomew; Thomas and Matthew the tax-collector; James son of Alphaeus, and Thaddaeus; Simon the Cananaean, and Judas Iscariot, the one who betrayed him. These twelve Jesus sent out with the following instructions: 'Go nowhere among the Gentiles, and enter no town of the Samaritans, but go rather to the lost sheep of the house of Israel. As you go, proclaim the good news, "The kingdom of heaven has come near."' (Matt. 10.1–7)

It was deeply ironic that the Gospel set for the opening day of the Transfiguring Episcope conference should be Matthew's account of the apostolic call, with its listing of the twelve male apostles. This passage confronts us not only with the challenge to proclaim that the kingdom of God is at hand, but also with

30

a vision of the authority given to those who are called to this ministry: 'authority over unclean spirits, to cast them out, and to cure every disease and every sickness'. At the same time, this is one of the central texts cited by those who argue that women are not called by God to the ordained ministry, and certainly not to the episcopate. This is where we learn the names of the twelve apostles who are deemed the model of ministry and the model of oversight: Simon called Peter, and Andrew, James the son of Zebedee and John, Philip and Bartholomew, Thomas and Matthew, James the son of Alphaeus and Thaddaeus, Simon and Judas.

They are indeed all men. They are also, as has often been pointed out, all Jewish, a criterion that was soon dropped as a criterion for becoming a Christian, and which probably never pertained to the ordained ministry at all. But what is truly extraordinary about this list is surely not that all of those included in it are men, but that they are all included. All these men are deemed by Christ worthy of the calling of apostle, of herald of the good news: Peter, who so often failed to understand what Jesus was trying to tell him; James and John, who so thoroughly misunderstood what Jesus was about that all they could think about was who would get the prized place at his right hand; Thomas, who would not believe until he had not only seen but touched (he gets a bad press as a doubter, but was Paul any better on this point?); Matthew, the tax collector whose very profession rendered him suspect to the people to whom he was sent to preach; Simon the Zealot, presumably some kind of freedom fighter or a terrorist; and Judas, who was going to betray him. That is the twelve: it is not exactly a group of men with outstanding leadership qualities and integrity. Rather, they could be seen as a group of misfits and failures. And yet they are all here in this list, charged with the proclamation of the gospel, sent out to do the work of the Lord.

There is something important and true here about the untidiness of the Church and the untidiness of leadership in the Church. Jesus doesn't subject the twelve to some kind of test of orthodoxy and right thinking before he sends them out. Instead, this group of people is sent to proclaim the coming of the kingdom, regardless of their betrayals and failures and shortcomings. They are sent out, imperfect as they are, to call and send others. It is not just despite but through their imperfections, through their awareness of weakness and the possibility of transformation, that the knowledge of the kingdom of God will be spread. The sending of the twelve is not about defining a little group of the super-elite, not about marking out an in-group, not about restriction of the proclamation of the gospel to a select few, but about the sending out of people who have encountered the living Christ in order that they may proclaim the good news of salvation to others, who will proclaim it to others in their turn. The important thing about these twelve who are called by Christ is not that they are men, but that they seem ready to be drawn into his mission: these are apostles who in their turn will call others to be apostles of Christ.

Matthew lists twelve men as those who share this responsibility, but one of the earliest biblical models for this pattern of apostolic ministry as sending is Mary Magdalene, witness to the resurrection, known in the early Church as the apostle to the apostles (*apostola apostolorum*).[1] The title was not restricted to her. Origen and Hippolytus of Rome refer not only to Mary Magdalene but to all the women at the tomb as well as the Samaritan woman at the well as apostles, because of their role in spreading the gospel.[2] However, only one woman is explicitly referred to in the New Testament as an apostle: Junia, praised, together with her companion Andronicus, by Paul as 'outstanding amongst the apostles' (Rom. 16.7).[3] John Chrysostom commented: 'How great is the wisdom of this woman, that she should be even counted worthy of the appellation of apostle!'[4] Writing a millennium later, Calvin explained in his commentary on Paul's greeting to Junia and Andronicus:

> Paul calls them *apostles*. He does not, however, use this word in its generally accepted sense, but extends it to include all those who do not just establish one church, but give their whole efforts to spreading the Gospel everywhere. In this

passage, therefore, Paul is referring to those who planted churches, by bringing the doctrine of salvation to various places, as apostles.[5]

Calvin goes on to suggest that Junia and Andronicus were the true founders of the church at Rome, on the basis that had Peter been in Rome, Paul would have included him in the list of greetings. Despite his own conviction that women may not preach or baptize, Calvin nonetheless perceives women as participating in the apostolic ministry of the early Church.

'The women of those days were more spirited than lions, sharing with the Apostles their labours for the Gospel's sake', commented John Chrysostom of Paul's greetings to women in Romans 16.[6] Women apostles continue to be attested – and so called – in the early Church. Thecla, the protagonist of the second-century *Acts of Paul and Thecla*, was long regarded as an apostle. Having heard Paul preach, Thecla rejects her fiancé in order to proclaim the gospel herself; when Paul refuses to baptize her – on the basis that she is too beautiful to persist in her preaching – she baptizes herself and is reluctantly accepted by Paul as his companion and fellow evangelist, accompanying him in his mission until she is finally martyred. Thecla was celebrated as an apostle by early church authors, was praised as a saint 'equal to the apostles' in Byzantine liturgy, and the *Acts* recounting her mission were regarded as canonical in some areas until into the sixth century.[7] Another early woman apostle of the third or fourth century, Nino, was the apostle to Georgia.[8] Taken captive by Georgian soldiers, Nino healed the sick, including the Queen of Georgia, who in gratitude persuaded her husband to be baptized.

It is well known that not all the church fathers were as enthusiastic about the work of such women as Chrysostom. From an early stage there was concern about recognizing women as preachers of the gospel and leaders within the Church. Around 200 CE, Tertullian commented disapprovingly of those who 'claim Thecla's example as a licence for women's teaching and baptizing'.[9] The *Didascalia Apostolorum*, written probably in the third century, thought that women should not teach, because 'the pagans will mock and scoff' if they hear the teaching of the incarnation and the resurrection from a woman; it also recommended that women should not baptize.[10] Writing in the fourth century, Epiphanius (c.315–403) saw women's leadership as a mark of a heretical church and insisted that Prisca (Rom. 16.3) and Junia (Rom. 16.7) must both be men, recounting that 'Junias' became bishop of Apamaea in Syria while 'Priscas' was bishop of Colophonos.[11] Epiphanius' recognition that Junia(s) and Prisca(s) shared in the apostolic ministry of proclaiming Christ's gospel not only led him to believe that they could not be women, but his conviction that the ministry of proclamation must be reserved to the clergy led him to consecrate these women bishops. Epiphanius is one example of the way in which the development of the episcopate brought about a sense that the proclamation of the gospel must be restricted to clergy, in contrast to the original sense that all were involved in the proclaiming of the gospel.

It is, however, entirely apparent that God did not stop calling women to proclaim the gospel just because the Church would not ordain them to do so. The lives of women martyrs and saints, however idealized, show the continuing witness of women for the gospel and their active involvement in the spread of Christianity. Moreover, the relatively few women's voices that have come down to us testify to their experience of being called, although they witness also to the difficulties many felt in accepting a call that the Church did not acknowledge, and show some of the ways in which women's sense of calling was shaped by the expectations of the Church.

Hildegard of Bingen (1098–1179) received her calling to teach and write through a vision:

I saw a great mountain the colour of iron, and enthroned on it One of such great glory that it blinded my sight . . . And behold, he who was enthroned upon that mountain cried out in a strong, loud voice saying, 'O human, who are fragile dust of the earth and ashes of ashes! Cry out and speak of the origin of pure salvation until those people are instructed who, although they see the inmost contents of the Scriptures, do not wish to tell them or speak them.'[12]

Hildegard initially felt unable to respond, but she was later granted another vision which encouraged her to speak and write despite her reservations:

Because you are timid about speaking and simple about explaining and unskilled about writing these things, speak and write those things not according to the mouth of a person, nor according to the perception of human inventiveness, nor according to the wishes of human arrangement, but according to the extent that you see and hear those things in the heavens above in the wonders of God.[13]

Writing to the Archbishop of Cologne, she reiterated the point that all that she offered was given her by God:

I – poor little woman that I am – sent my book of truthful visions to you, just as you requested. I remind you that it contains nothing originating from human wisdom nor from my own will, but rather it contains those truths which the unfailing Light wished to reveal through his own words. Indeed, this very letter which I am now writing to you came in a similar manner, not from my intellect nor through any human mediation, but through divine revelation.[14]

Hildegard would become one of the most respected theological teachers of her age, abbess of an important monastery, consulted by politicians and bishops, embarking on three tours during which she would speak to crowds of thousands gathered outside churches. These were not preaching tours, for as a woman Hildegard was not allowed to preach, but scripture taught that women might prophesy ('Your sons and daughters will prophesy, your old men will dream dreams, your young men will see visions' – Joel 2.28; Acts 2.17), and prophesy she did, in ways that looked remarkably like the sermons of her day.

In her work *The Flowing Light of the Godhead*, German Beguine Mechthild of Magdeburg (1210–*c*.1285) gives a moving account of her sense of being called into a deeper relationship with God:

> The Lord invites the soul to dance:
> I cannot dance, Lord, unless you lead me.
> If you want me to leap with abandon,
> You must intone the song.
> Then I shall leap into love,
> From love into knowledge,
> From knowledge into enjoyment,
> And from enjoyment beyond all human sensations.
> There I want to remain, yet want also to circle higher still.[15]

Mechthild clearly had a deep wish to understand and know God better, and she was also convinced that not only had she been called into such a relationship with God, she was mature and ready for it: 'That is child's love, that one suckle and rock a baby. I am a full-grown bride. I want to go to my Lover',[16] she reprimands the soul's senses when they have suggested that she picture herself caring for the infant Jesus. Mechthild nonetheless felt the need to justify her writing about the knowledge of God that had been revealed to her, not least because she received severe criticism for having done so:

> I was warned against writing this book.
> People said: if one did not watch out, it could be burned.
> So I did as I used to do as a child.
> When I was sad, I always had to pray.
> I bowed to my Lover and said: 'Alas, Lord,
> now I am saddened all because of your honour.
> If I am going to receive no comfort from you now,
> then you led me astray,
> Because you are the one who told me to write it.'

36

At once God revealed himself to my joyless soul, held this
book in his right hand, and said: 'My dear one, do not be
overly troubled,
No one can burn the truth . . .
The words symbolize my marvellous Godhead.
It flows continuously into your soul from my divine mouth.
The sound of the words is a sign of my living spirit
and through it achieves genuine truth.
Now examine all these words –
How admirably do they proclaim my personal secrets!
So have no doubts about yourself.'
[*Mechthild:*] 'Ah, Lord, if I were a learned religious man,
and if you had performed this unique miracle using him,
you would receive everlasting honour for it.
But how is one supposed to believe
that you have built a golden house on filthy ooze . . .
Lord, earthly wisdom will not be able to find you there.'
[*God replies:*] '. . . One finds many a professor learned in
scripture who actually is a fool in my eyes.
And I'll tell you something else:
It is a great honour for me with regard to them, and it very
much strengthens Holy Christianity that the unlearned tongue,
aided by my Holy Spirit, teaches the learned tongue.'[17]

Mechthild wrote much of her work while she was a Beguine,
at the suggestion of her confessor. Some time around 1270 she
entered the Cistercian community at Helfta under the leadership
of Gertrude the Great, herself a renowned spiritual leader, warn-
ing them before her arrival: 'You want to have instruction from
me, but I myself am uneducated. What you are searching for you
can find a thousand times better in your books.'[18] Nonetheless,
she soon became drawn into instructing the nuns. Mechthild's
calling had led her to teach and to proclaim the gospel that was
revealed to her despite opposition.

Marguerite Porète, who was burned as a heretic in 1310, articulated a very clear wish that others would find God through
her:

37

And so this poor suppliant creature wrote what you hear; and it was her wish that her neighbours would find God in her, through her writings and her words . . . and in doing this, and saying this, and willing this, a suppliant she remained, know this well, and burdened down by herself; and she was a suppliant because this was what she wished to do.[19]

Porète was burned because her words were deemed heretical, but her work lived on as an instruction manual frequently used for instruction within the most orthodox communities.[20] Although she did not live to see it, Marguerite's wish that others would find God through her was fulfilled.

Julian of Norwich (1342–c.1416) was aware of her limitations as a woman, and on one level denied any claim to be a teacher: 'But God forbid that you should say or take it so that I am a teacher, for I do not mean so. No, I never meant so. For I am a woman, unlearned, feeble and frail.'[21] What she could and did affirm was that she was teaching only what she had received from God, and this she had from love of God and neighbour to pass on, regardless of the fact that she was a woman:

I have it of the Showing of him who is sovereign teacher. But truly charity stirs me to tell you it. For I would God were known and my even-Christians helped, as I would be myself, to the more hating of sin and loving of God. But because I am a woman, should I therefore believe that I should not tell you the goodness of God?

The point is not that Julian should be better known, but that those who hear should 'behold Jesus who is the teacher of all'.[22] Julian was at pains also to affirm her orthodoxy and her knowledge of the faith as taught by the Church as well as directly from God:

in all things I believe as holy Church believes, preaches and teaches, for the faith of holy Church, of which I had understanding beforehand and, as I hope by the grace of God, wilfully kept in use and custom, stood continually in my sight, willing and meaning never to receive anything that might be contrary thereunto.[23]

A century after Julian's death, the Reformation burst on to the German scene, bringing a new sense of urgency to the proclamation of the word of God. However, Reformers were not always gratified when women responded to the call just as much as men. The Bavarian noblewoman Argula von Grumbach (1492–c.1554) published an open letter in defence of a Lutheran student in Ingolstadt, and was criticized not only for her theological views but for her temerity, in speaking out on such matters as a woman. Her response to the poem consisted of a comprehensive biblical justification of her right to speak. An important passage for her is Joel's conviction that sons and daughters will prophesy: the inspiration of the Spirit, she concludes, cannot be restricted to men alone.[24] This reading is confirmed by Paul, who reveals everyone to be a temple of the Spirit.[25] Equally, John records Christ's invitation to all who thirst for him: 'Come unto me!'[26] This excludes neither peasants nor women; indeed, she comments, the first disciple was a fisherman.[27] Similarly, Mark records that all are called to preach.[28] Von Grumbach goes on to cite cases where women have acted or spoken to bring about God's word: Judith's assassination of Holofernes,[29] Jael's assassination of Sisera[30] and, somewhat less bloodily, Deborah's status as prophet, seer and judge.[31] Finally she notes that even a donkey can reveal God's word on occasion, as shown by Balaam's ass – and if a donkey may speak God's word, surely so too may a woman.[32]

Argula von Grumbach was silenced when her husband was removed from his post. Katharina Schütz Zell, wife of the sixteenth-century reformer Matthias Zell, also felt a strong need to proclaim the gospel, which drove her to publish a defence of her marriage to a priest and a letter of encouragement to women whose husbands had been forced into exile. She was silenced by Strasbourg's reforming council, but found her own way of preaching the gospel of the love of God through care for the

39

prisoners and exiles, the sick and the dying.[33] Katharina Schütz Zell's example may have been one of the reasons why Calvin could recognize the role of Junia in proclaiming the gospel in Rome.

'Because I am a woman, should I therefore believe that I should not tell you the goodness of God?' asks Julian of Norwich. Her question is, sadly, still pertinent today, but it articulates the deep sense of calling felt by women through the ages as they responded to the imperative of the gospel. The restriction of Matthew's list to twelve men has never been enough to prevent women receiving and responding to God's call. Through the ages the authority promised to those who receive God's call has rested upon women as well as men. Women too have obeyed the missionary command: 'As you go, proclaim the good news, "The kingdom of heaven has come near!"'

4

SOME REFLECTIONS ON WOMEN AND LEADERSHIP IN ANGLICAN RELIGIOUS COMMUNITIES

Sr Anita Cook

Most people in the Anglican Communion do not know that there are communities of Anglican religious, sisters and brothers, nuns and monks. One sister, from the All Saints Sisters of the Poor in the United States, was told authoritatively by a woman in a parish where she was giving a talk that she couldn't possibly be an Episcopal Sister. She had been seriously misinformed; there were no such things as Anglican/Episcopal Sisters!

We, like most Anglican religious communities, have a history of strong, able women, who pioneered ministry in many parts of the world as well as the UK. Anglican religious communities came into being during the Victorian era. Despite the fact that there was a woman on the throne, the prevailing attitude was that women needed men to be in charge and to organize any enterprise. The idea of women in a leadership position was not an acceptable concept. As Peter Anson in his classic *The Call of the Cloister* points out, one of the reasons the bishops at the time were opposed to women taking vows of celibacy was the fact that then they would not be available for marriage, which was, as they saw it, the primary function of women.[1] Peta Dunstan in her historical summary in the most recent (2004) edition of *A Handbook of the Religious Life*[2] shows how after the Lambeth Conference of 1897 bishops tried to gain control over religious orders, particularly those for women, as they experienced them as outside their control. This was the beginning of the history of what is now the Advisory Council on the Relations of Bishops and Religious Communities in the Church of England. Several of the overseas provinces have a comparable body. Relationships have moved on and at the last two Lambeth Conferences there have been meetings for bishops from around the Communion, who are involved in various ways with members of religious communities, some of whom have been members of the chaplaincy team.

Women in Victorian days might have been allowed some say in the running of a household, but it was the husband or father who ruled and controlled the finances. It is still predominantly the attitude towards women in the Solomon Islands though the reasons there are cultural. At a deep level some men are threatened by women ably running their own affairs without them. For a number of men and some women, St Paul's headship argument means that only men should be in charge and have oversight. Caroline Walker Bynum's work reflecting on what happened at a much earlier time, when even women monastics were controlled by the clergy, showed how some nuns, by becoming acclaimed as holy, which was proved by abnormal physical signs, were able to gain a degree of independence and freedom from clerical domination.[3]

In 1870 Emily Ayckbowm felt called by God to found the Community of the Sisters of the Church, of which I am a member. I have recently stepped down from having served 11 years in both the overall international leadership role and as UK Provincial. All the other women's communities founded in the early period, apart from the Society of the Sisters of Bethany and ourselves, had as their founder an influential priest. William Butler, Vicar of Wantage, founded the Community of St Mary the

Virgin, which is now the oldest surviving Anglican community. Canon Carter, Vicar of Clewer, founded the Community of St John the Baptist, and the famous Dr John Mason Neal of East Grinstead, the Society of St Margaret. The latter was actually inhibited, at the time when he founded them, one of the reasons being that he was enabling women to join a community. All these founders became wardens of their communities and all wrote, or in the case of Carter heavily contributed to, the Rule by which others – namely each community, and not themselves – lived. They obviously would not have succeeded without the leadership and co-operation of the women in those communities at the time, but there was no doubt as to the ultimate authority of the father founder, especially in a community's early life.

Emily was a woman of her time, but did not subscribe to the view that 'men know best' and although she was a great respecter of people, be they children, people in need of various sorts, priests or bishops, she did not lose her critical faculties. Perhaps being raised in a clergy household and having a brother who was a priest led to her seeing clergy very much as ordinary fallible human beings. One of the controversial issues of the day was the caring for 'foundling children', those who were illegitimate and abandoned on convent doorsteps. It was seen by the great and the good as 'encouraging vice'. The then Archbishop of Canterbury, Benson, wanted to visit CSC and persuade Emily to abide by his findings and recommendations. Emily politely declined and just removed his name from the list of Patrons. Benson described her as 'the most comically audacious Mother in the universe'.

'Pro ecclesia Dei', interpreted as 'For the whole people of God', is the motto chosen by Emily for the community. Its purpose was to 'promote the honour and glory of Almighty God and the extension of His kingdom on earth'. She chose for our patrons the Archangel Michael and All the Angels, reminding the community of our call to adoration and action. The call is to live life in community, rooted in corporate and personal prayer and to live that God-centredness out in daily life by an active ministry of serving others. The purpose is that others may come to know the living, loving God. She was a strong believer in education,

43

the care of orphans and the marginalized. She believed in enabling and equipping women to deal with the various situations in which they found themselves. This formed one of the main thrusts of the community's work and mission.

By the time of her death in 1900 the community was established not only in England but in Canada, Australia, New Zealand, India and South Africa. Today we have four provinces: the UK, Australia, Canada and the Solomon Islands. We function as one community with an overall leader and a general chapter. Each province also has its own provincial and chapter. In some ways we experience some of the difficulties of the Anglican Communion. To what extent can we function as one body, and how do we incorporate and respect the different cultural needs? How do we as a whole body make decisions and live them out? How do we learn from each other's experiences?

I am a strong believer that the different contributions and viewpoints that each nation brings to the whole body enriches it. In our case, because one of our Canadian sisters, Benedetta, felt called to ordination as a priest, the whole community debated the question of women's ordination long before it became an option in Australia or England.

The Canadian Church was the first to ordain women legally, the whole process being worked through discerningly, gently and carefully under the wise leadership of the then Primate Ted Scott. As a community it meant that we were all enriched by the Canadian experience. There were three sisters who were opposed at the time of the first ordinations in Canada but God called them to himself and it has not been an issue since. The sisters in Canada and those who visited were used to experiencing women functioning as priests and more latterly as bishops. Having spent 16 years in Canada myself, I found it hard on my return to think myself into the space where I could appreciate the difficulties that some of the communities and religious here in the UK felt and feel.

Currently we have four functioning ordained members, two in the UK and two in Australia, Benedetta now being retired. Our sisters in the Solomons are looking forward hopefully to the possibility of sisters there being ordained. The thinking is that having sisters ordained first will open up the possibility for other women there. Although there is a questionable aspect to this approach, working within the culture and being able to let people have the experience will move people on in an acceptable way. Women from overseas can and do preside there, but experiencing one of their own women who happens to be a sister will be different.

Making progress regarding the ordination of women in the Solomons has been difficult as it is counter-cultural in what is mostly a patriarchal society. We are not there yet, despite the valiant efforts of Archbishop Ellison Pogo. One of the great blessings of the Lambeth Conference was to have all the Melanesian bishops, plus visitors, plus English diocesans all gathered together in one place for some time. It made it possible to work out a way forward.

The idea does not seem to register, that the whole Communion can be enriched by the work a particular province or diocese has done. Here in England, most of the time people know little if anything of what is happening elsewhere. The prevailing attitude seems to be 'it doesn't happen if it doesn't happen here'. Yes, there will be cultural differences, but we could all further the work of the gospel, if we were sensible and humble enough to learn from each other. Currently the Diocese of Melbourne in Australia has taken the issue of 'bullying' in the Church seriously and has set up a process for working with the issue to bring about change. Most of the Church of England seems to be in denial that it exists.

Leadership in the past was very much in the hierarchical mode. In the time of Hildegard of Bingen, abbesses within their own abbeys had the same power as abbots, other than not being ordained. The mother superior was the authority within the community and its various works. As the works of the communities multiplied and spread overseas, it was necessary and inevitable that those on the ground, in the front line, had to use their own initiative. This enabled various enterprises to flourish, as letters to and from the far-flung outposts of the then Empire took time to arrive. Most of the undertakings would probably have died with today's instant communication networks, as permissions would need to be asked for and might not be given. In medieval times the sister on the spot had to make decisions, rather than their being made by someone who could not appreciate the local circumstances.

When I was blessed into Office, our then Visitor Bishop Dr Peter Selby gave a homily, looking at the positive and negative interpretations of the words 'leader and mother'. He finished by saying that there was also the question of 'followership' and his experience of us as a group was that we elected people into leadership and then did everything in our power to resist being led. This is true not only within the confines of our community but also in the wider Church and society. We are living in an age where broadly speaking there is no 'positional authority'. The fact that one might have been chosen, selected or elected to a role, these days does not mean that people will be prepared to follow your lead on a matter, even though they may have voted for you.

I assumed Office on 1 March, the feast of St David. I chose as the Gospel John 21.15–19, which has always been significant to me on my faith journey. It is also, as Bishop Peter remarked, one of the Gospels used at the consecration of a bishop and as such it was suited to a new leader of a community taking Office. For me at the time, Jesus' three requests to Peter – 'Feed my lambs', 'Tend my sheep', 'Feed my sheep' – felt like God's call to me at different stages on my faith journey: to be a teacher, to come to religious life, and the call to leadership in it. Further into my time, the call to ordained ministry resurfaced and this I came to see was my third call to ministry. Much to my surprise I was enabled to be ordained while I was still in Office. The experience of ordination and being able to preside, as we as community gathered around the altar both here and overseas, was a very powerful one and remains so though now it has a different dynamic.

Today the task of leadership in our whole society, particularly in the Church, is fraught with difficulty because in our more individualistic society people expect to be able not only to have a voice but also a vote in the decision-making process. The notion of followership, of being able to voice your views but to support what emerges as being best for the whole body rather than your individual preference, seems on the whole to be an 'alien' concept. We in our western culture are continually being asked for our opinion across a whole host of matters, from voting in the *X Factor* to whether or not we should have gone to war in Iraq and everything in between. People expect to be consulted but also have their opinion agreed with. 'You are not hearing me' can be a way of stating annoyance that you are not agreeing with the other's opinion. How much should protests decide government policy? Politicians work to give us the choice of the market place in education and in health care, so we in the Church come to expect a wide range of choice.

It has been said that the Church is not a democracy, but particularly now, I think, there is a feeling that it should be. The notion that Anglican polity is a Church that is 'synodically governed and episcopally led' is an idea that plays out differently in different dioceses, provinces and national churches, let alone different cultures and nations. Some bishops have different ideas about synodical government. How bishops are chosen – elected or appointed – varies across the Communion. The relationships between bishops and their synods differ enormously. People in the Communion and the Church feel that if their views or interpretations differ from the main body's decision, then the main body has a moral duty to make provision for their particular needs within it.

Another factor shaping our leadership is the increasing loss of Anglican identity. Anglican identity is hard to define: it is wide and broad, but it does exist. It was palpable at the 2008 Lambeth Conference that we were all part of the same family, despite some strong opposing views. Increasingly there are a number of people coming into leadership both in religious communities and in ordained ministry whose knowledge and experience of being an Anglican is limited. This is good in bringing in new ideas and fresh ways of thinking, but has its downside when it comes to knowing who we are.

47

Being a woman in leadership, particularly in relating to men, still has its challenges. It is difficult to know how much it is a question of different personalities, but my observation and experience is that women must work much harder than men to be heard in debates. An observation when talking with some of the women bishops present at Lambeth from the Episcopal Church was that although relations regarding women in the Episcopate is complex, some women bishops were experienced as being more considerate and respectful of the needs of those who objected to their leadership than some of their male counterparts.

A religious community, like a local parish community, can often mirror some of the wider problems of trying to be 'the body of Christ' in this place and time. When you move into the scene of a province you encounter the realm of competing needs for limited resources. When you move into the wider international scene you encounter the need to understand different cultural ways of operating. A religious community is a voluntary society of consenting adults. The individual feels drawn by God to join this particular group. The group, initially through its leadership, will decide whether or not to invite this person in to explore their vocation in this community. If the person is in the right place to grow into fullness of life, then they will progress through the various stages into full membership. But it is a closed group, unlike a good parish.

Being a member of this closed group, opting to commit yourself to living out your life, your Christian life, in this particular framework of gospel living, defined by its Rule and constitution, does make the whole experience more intense. The usual escape and avoidance routes are not available, even though as religious we can usually come up with some. It is a way of life that is 24/7, though these days there is holiday time and free days.

There was in our community a strong feeling with some that we as a particular group of women should be able to find all the resources for our life and development as a community within our own ranks. Sometimes we might have people come to give input in various areas, such as biblical study or spirituality, and the idea that we needed outside expertise to help us see how we were functioning as a body and as an organization, and whether or not we were focused and striving towards our prime task, was in some cases strongly resisted and in others people just did not see the need. The same thing happens in the Church, not only provincially but in the wider Communion. We do not draw on each other's expertise and resources in different areas or use the resources available within our own cultures. Naturally all the usual group dynamics also come into play, like denial. The 'elephant in the room' at a meeting looking at the future and leadership in the Church of England was being ignored, with no one mentioning the issue of women in the episcopate here.

Anglican communities have a strong resistance to what might be seen as outside interference – Emily Ayckbourn and Archbishop Benson provide one example. There was a real reason for it then, but in many ways communities have moved from the edge into being part of the establishment, with all the pluses and minuses of that position. Members can confuse flexibility and the need to be accountable, to assess what is happening both within the closed group and within the wider Christian community and society, with not being loyal to the foundation values of religious life, or in some cases not being loyal to the leader. There can be, in my view, the fatal contentedness of feeling that we are all right as we are, we are comfortable and only want challenges to come in certain acceptable ways. There is a tendency for the focus to be internal rather than being able to stand back and see the bigger picture and to discover new ways of telling the good news of God's love in a way that communicates with where people are now.

In order to bring in God's realm today with the particular group we belong to we are all called to be responsible for making our contribution to the whole. We need to recognize the distinctive role not only of the designated leader/s but the part each one of us plays. It no longer works from the 'top down'. People need to be engaged and brought onside. People say they want leadership that articulates a vision and they sincerely mean that. What is not on the whole realized is that often people want the vision to resonate with what *they* think it should be, even though they

49

don't know what that is. The charismatic leader comes and goes. What is needed is the empowerment of the whole ongoing body and all its members. The corporate body needs to be willing to make decisions for the benefit of the whole not only within this particular group but for the wider world in which we all live and are called to serve. Together we need to be willing to make decisions and also to implement them. In a real way leadership is followership, discerning what God is doing and saying in the gathered community. Followership is also leadership in the ongoing group, each one taking responsibility for discerning and sharing the way forward. Together as followers of Jesus we seek to bring in God's realm here on earth now.

PART 2

LEADERSHIP AND ECCLESIASTICAL AUTHORITY

5
REFLECTIONS ON WOMEN, AUTHORITY AND THE CHURCH FROM AN AMERICAN PERSPECTIVE

Catherine S. Roskam

The Episcopal Church is an 'international church'. We have for some time now dropped the name ECUSA, as our dioceses are drawn together into one Anglican province from 14 different countries. Nevertheless, I am aware that my experience in the Church has been distinctly North American, shaped in the context of US culture, and it is from this perspective that I offer the following reflections on my own experience, on women and the Church, on patriarchy, and on a possible way forward.

A personal history

When I was ordained priest in 1984, women's ordination was no longer such a controversial issue, at least in the Diocese of New York where I was working. Discrimination in the ordination

53

process seemed to have evaporated and first placements as curates and assistants were fairly easy to come by. However, while people were comfortable with women in some kind of assisting position, they preferred their rectors to be male. In those days I would read my seminary class news to find to my dismay that after two or three years my male classmates were becoming rectors while I and my female counterparts were either remaining in an assisting position or being placed in charge of small missions, often at less than full-time compensation, or else deployed as chaplains.[1]

In 1989, after five years as an assistant in a New York City parish, my family and I moved to California in hopes that the situation might be different there, but the story was pretty much the same. We had a strong women's clergy group, though, for mutual support and much laughter. Some of us formed a sub-group called 'The Seconds Club' because so many of us had come in second in search processes, losing positions of rector or priest-in-charge to less experienced male counterparts. Vestries could recognize our gifts for ministry and even enjoy our company, but somehow in the end could not bring themselves to live with the profound discomfort gender difference seemed to promise in the one to be in charge.[2]

The last time I came in second was in June 1990. Having had six solid years of parish experience as an assistant rector and as an interim rector, and having given a really good interview, I nevertheless lost the position to a young male priest, two years out of seminary, who though he showed a lot of promise, had no comparable parish experience.[3]

For me spiritually and emotionally, it felt like God's last straw. I flew back to the east coast to go on retreat at the Society of St John the Evangelist, where I have been an associate since 1981. I was in the midst of some heavy conversations with God in which I was questioning the divine wisdom in calling me to a priesthood I was not going to be able to exercise fully, when my retreat was interrupted by a phone call from the deployment officer back in California. It seemed there was a small mission church in San Francisco whose vicar had just died after a prolonged illness. The recent earthquake had damaged the roof so

54

there was some danger of it falling in. Only twelve people attended Sunday service. Five out of the six who served on the bishop's committee had voted to close. The bishop was wisely refusing to move on closure while the congregation was still grieving for their vicar. He needed someone to go in and work with them for a few months to see if any viability remained. And by the way, it wasn't clear how they felt about women priests. Would I be interested?

Oddly, it sounded like a call to me, so I said, 'Sure!' Nine months later, the church had a new roof in place and about 50 or 60 people on a Sunday morning. No one talked about closing any more and somehow they had forgotten that I was a woman priest. I was just a priest who happened also to be a woman.

The Bishop of California then invited me to join his staff as Missioner of the Diocese.[4] The position was episcopal in nature, since I had oversight of 24 congregations and a yearly rota of visitation. Five years as missioner was excellent training for being a bishop, although I did not think about it that way at the time. Becoming a bishop was simply not on my radar screen. So I was quite surprised in 1995 to learn that someone had submitted my name for consideration as Suffragan in the Diocese of New York. In the Episcopal Church suffragans, like diocesan bishops, are elected by the diocese they will serve. I was elected at a special convention held on 10 June 1995. In the first ballot I came in second. I can remember praying in St James Chapel of the Cathedral of St John the Divine, in New York City, where the convention was being held, and saying to God that if I came in second, as I had done in so many priestly searches, it would be fine. It had been an enriching search process and I was perfectly happy to remain in California. But my numbers climbed steadily on the second and third ballots and I was elected on the fourth.

Under Richard Grein, the diocesan at the time of my election, I served as a regional bishop, serving the middle region of the diocese. Under his successor, Mark Sisk, the fifteenth Bishop of New York, I still retain oversight of the congregations in that region, but I also oversee congregational development and other matters and do visitations throughout the whole diocese.

55

I have been ordained for 25 years and am now in the fourteenth year of my consecration as a bishop – the fourth woman in the Episcopal Church and the fifth in the Anglican Communion to hold such office.

Despite the deployment difficulties in my early years as a priest, in terms of ordination itself, both as a priest and a bishop, I am part of the 'second wave'.[5] I did not have to endure the discrimination nor was I subject to the indignities suffered by some of my sisters. For example, the three women bishops consecrated before me had protests at their consecration services. Barbara Harris, the first woman bishop in both the Episcopal church and the Anglican Communion, had no fewer than three protests at her consecration and even received death threats. I suffered none of that, nor did the women who came after me.

In the early years of my consecration, much was made of my being a 'woman bishop', albeit mostly in positive ways, but that is no longer the case. To the congregations I visit I am simply the one of the three New York bishops who happens to be a woman. I feel very blessed in this regard.[6]

Women in the Episcopal Church

Much has changed in the Episcopal Church since the advent of women's ordination in 1976. Now finally women really are being called as rectors or priests-in-charge of larger congregations. The first woman bishop was a suffragan, but the second was elected diocesan. To what factors can we attribute this progress?

First, the unsung heroes of the advancement of ordained women in the Church are the male rectors who insisted on hiring women assistants, often over the objections of their vestries.[7] What congregations found was that, with very few exceptions, they grew to love and respect those women priests and in fact over time began not to notice the gender difference as much as they had expected, except in ways that were positive. In my own experience, families with daughters have often shared with me how important it is for them to see a woman 'up front'.

Pastorally, women sometimes come to women priests and bishops with matters considered too delicate or intimate to be shared with a man.

Second, women who were deployed by bishops to care for small and struggling congregations did some extraordinary work in congregational growth and development in those contexts and the rest of the church began to take notice, wooing them away to larger congregations.

Third, exposure to women priests and bishops has increasingly conditioned people, especially younger generations, to think of clergy as both male and female. Indeed, a male colleague told me that a little boy in a parish previously visited by a woman bishop was startled to see him at their next visitation. The boy was reported to have turned to his mother in surprise and asked her, 'Can boys be bishops too?'

Fourth, and I know this will be controversial in some contexts, ordained women owe a great deal, albeit indirectly, to the gay rights movement. I have often said, not entirely in jest, that I owe my ordination to Stonewall, the 1969 uprising of gay, lesbian and transgendered persons that marked the beginning of the gay pride movement. As gay men came to accept themselves and live openly as gay, what is referred to in the United States as 'coming out of the closet', misogyny dissipated. This was especially true of the Church. Misogyny is the handmaiden of 'the closet'. Space does not allow for the discussion this deserves, but conscience does not permit me to omit its mention.

And yet for all the progress with regard to the ordination of women over the last three decades, deployment data from the Church Pension Group and surveys taken by the Committee on the Status of Women, a committee of the Executive Council of the Episcopal Church, have repeatedly demonstrated that while there has been significant progress in women's deployment in some dioceses of the Episcopal Church, overall women clergy are still underemployed and underpaid in comparison to their male counterparts, with only a few exceptions.[8] In a report to the 75th General Convention in 2006, as part of the commemoration of the thirtieth anniversary of the decision to ordain women made at the 65th General Convention in 1976, the Committee on the Status of Women reported that:

> The Church has approximately 1,700 women priests serving in active full-time ministry and hundreds of others in part-time work, many honed and deepened by years of experience as priests in the church. However, women have yet to be regarded as serious candidates for many of the largest parishes in most dioceses, and the numbers of women elected bishop are disproportionately low, less than ten per cent of the total number.

Why is this so? And why, even in dioceses that strongly embrace the idea of women's ordination, are women still under-deployed as rectors and priests-in-charge? I would like to suggest that the core issue is not women's ordination but women's authority and the perception of women's power.

In her indispensable book *Talking from 9 to 5: How Women's and Men's Conversational Styles Affect Who gets Heard, Who Gets Credit, and What Gets Done at Work*,[9] Deborah Tannen points out that our primary images of female authority come from motherhood.

> The prospect of a man checking with a woman before doing something . . . [brings to mind] the scenario of a child supplicant, because a mother is one of the few images we have of female authority – whereas men in authority are as likely to suggest a military commander or a sports coach or captain (in itself modeled on the military metaphor) as a father.[10]

Tannen points to the work of applied linguist Elinor Ochs in comparing the way mothers talk to their children in 'mainstream white middle class homes' in the USA as compared to traditional Samoan households:

> Ochs shows that because of the Americans' egalitarian ideology, they tend to downplay their own power and authority

58

relative to their children. Many facets of the hierarchical organization of Samoan society give power and authority to women in the role of mother.[11]

In a further discussion of the image of authority, Tannen says:

> Part of the reason images of women in positions of authority are marked by their gender is that the very notion of authority is associated with maleness. This can result simply from appearance. Anyone who is taller, more heftily built, with a lower-pitched, more sonorous voice, begins with culturally recognized markers of authority, whereas anyone who is shorter, slighter, with a higher-pitched voice begins with a disadvantage in this respect.[12]

Clothes play a part also, as Tannen so aptly articulates, to 'mark' a woman in a particular way. With a small group of men and women gathered for a conference she notes:

> I was able to identify the styles and types of the women at the conference because each of us had to make decisions about hair, clothing, makeup and accessories, and each of those decisions carried meaning. Every style available to us was marked. Of course, the men in our group had to make decisions too, but their choices carried far less meaning. The men could have chosen styles that were marked, but they didn't have to, and in this group, none did. Unlike the women, they had the option of being unmarked . . . All eight men wore brown or blue slacks and standard-style shirts of light colors.[13]
>
> No man wore sandals or boots; their shoes were dark, closed, comfortable and flat. In short, unmarked. Although no man wore make-up, you couldn't say the men didn't wear make-up in the sense that you could say a woman didn't wear make-up. For men, no make-up is unmarked. I asked myself what style we women could have adopted that would have been unmarked, like the men's. The answer was: none. There is no unmarked woman.

59

Tannen writes about the world of business, but the same holds true for the Church. Liturgical dress is historically (and blessedly!) unisex, but clericals are men's clothing. And we women clergy are most definitely 'marked' by how we mix that men's shirt and collar with the rest of our wardrobe. Marking by its very nature undercuts the perception of authority, as it sets us apart from what is considered normative or neutral. What is normative would engender no comment. It is this often unconscious understanding of male authority as normative that gave rise to The Seconds Club, as people who ardently supported women's ordination showed by their choices that they did not approve or at least did not feel comfortable with women's authority.

Although some progress towards gender balance in the Church and in society has been made in the last three and a half decades, it is fair to say that most of our authority figures and power-brokers are still male: boards, CEOs, presidents, congress, investment bankers; and in the Church, bishops, priests and deans, both of seminaries and of cathedrals, with few exceptions.

And finally, even when women break through barriers and assume positions of authority, they pay an inordinate emotional price. As the report to the 2006 General Convention of the Commission on the Status of Women states:

There is also an awareness among women who have been ordained for many years that serving as a priest in a patriarchal institution can take a substantial emotional and physical toll on women. This becomes increasingly obvious the longer the woman participates in active ministry, and it is particularly acute as retirement issues are faced.

This may account at least in part for the reason why so many qualified women are reluctant to put their names forward in episcopal searches in the USA. While studies among younger generations show a trend away from the expectation of male dominance and towards the expectation of a more egalitarian society, that trend will be nurtured only by the continuity of experience of women in leadership roles.

Patriarchy

Patriarchy is the institutional expression of the belief that maleness is normative for the human race and that females are something less than fully human. Aristotle put it another way: that women are 'unfinished men'. The premise that maleness is normative for the human race has shaped almost every aspect of western civilization: art, government, education, Church. While these systems are beginning to change, all of us nevertheless participate in patriarchal systems even though few of us would consciously espouse the premise upon which patriarchy is based.

Feminism, by contrast, makes no claim that femaleness is normative for the human race, but rather and simply that women are indeed fully human. Few people would disagree with this statement out loud in public, and yet they act out this denial of women's full humanity, consciously or unconsciously, principally by denying women agency. If women have no agency then they can have no authority.

Agency as male provenance and privilege is a notion based in a mistaken perception of human biology: that is, that the male is sole genitor while the female is solely the vessel. While the female might nourish the seed planted within her with her own substance, she has no part in the agency of that life.

Science has shown us that this is not true, that the female contributes an equal and necessary part to the equation of new life. That leaves those of us in the Church with a special dilemma, since much of our formulation of God as Father is based on this misunderstanding, as is the traditional formulation of the Holy Trinity.

Patriarchal thinking breaks down not only in the light of scientific knowledge, but also theologically in the question of what it means to be made in the image of God. If we women do not have agency by nature of our sex, then we cannot be made in the image of God, as scripture tells us in Genesis 1.27. For in what respect is humanity made in the image of God? It is not in our biology. That is part of our creatureliness. But rather it is in our consciousness, our compassion, our creativity (including agency), our ability to communicate by word, and above all our ability to love. The gravitational pull towards relationship is the action of the Holy Trinity, God in loving, creative relationship within the Godhead, at work within us.

No supportable theological grounding exists for opposition to women's ordination, to women's agency, or by extrapolation, to women's authority.

The way forward for women in the Church

Some of the more radical rhetoric of feminism is to reject patriarchy in all its aspects. Not only is that not possible, since patriarchy permeates every aspect of our society, but also it is not a good idea. Patriarchy has brought culture and civilization many gifts, and we ought not to throw the proverbial baby out with the bathwater.

First, let us look for a moment at the matter of language. Not many people in churches today object to more inclusive language when it pertains to humanity. Changes in the English language, especially in American English, render 'men' an archaic and inadequate term to represent all of humanity, both female and male. 'Brothers and sisters', 'humanity', 'people', 'human beings', 'mortals' are all terms much more in keeping with original intent and meaning than a current understanding of the word 'man'.

The controversy lies in God language. Let us look for a moment at the growing trend in the USA to replace the traditional formulation of the Trinity as Father, Son and Holy Spirit, with formulations such as Creator, Redeemer, Sanctifier. Certainly God in all three persons of the Trinity creates, redeems and sanctifies, but this formulation at worst risks an understanding of the Trinity as three persons each with a different function and at best simply does not get to the relational essence of Trinitarian theology.

It is true that the imagery of the orthodox formulation of the Trinity is excessively male. How, you might ask, can a feminist,

62

who understands women to be as fully human as the men, bless with this exclusively male imagery, or recite the Creed for that matter? I believe the answer is to say these words as the ancients meant them, and not as modern science has revealed them. God the Father signifies God as the Genitor of all that is. Jesus is 'his only son', in the Hebrew sense of 'bar' meaning 'of the same substance as'. Paul tells us that we are all 'sons of God by adoption', meaning participating in the same substance and also that we are heirs, whether we are men or women. In Christ there is no male or female after all.[14]

Our challenge in this postmodern twenty-first century is to release the white-knuckled grasp of literalism. Church fathers were much more fluid in their thinking about gender and the divine than we are. Gregory of Nyssa in the fourth century had no trouble imaging God as Mother-in-law to the bridal couple of Jesus and his bride, the Church. So we must also sit loosely with the term Father. God is not a man. God is God. And because we must sit loosely with the term Father, we must also help the Church to sit more loosely with feminine terms, like Mother, as our forebears did, and to use more of the myriad names of God we find in our scripture and tradition.

Second, let us consider the issue of authority. In the USA, women are often reluctant to claim the authority that is rightfully theirs, no doubt in part because of American egalitarian ideology. Beyond that, it is my experience, very much in keeping with Deborah Tannen's observations, that women themselves view exercising authority as unfeminine. There is much talk about the leadership style of women as circular, relational and shared, with no one exercising authority over another. My experience of leadership circles is that they are excellent as exercises to deepen sharing and to get a sense of the group as a whole, but leaderless anything is a guarantee of failure. I have never known any organization based solely on these methods to last more than a few years. Put another way, leadership is everything. Women need to claim their authority and rise to the challenge, not to reproduce the autocracy of 'father knows best', but to exercise the bold, compassionate, inclusive, empowering leadership to which God has called us.

And finally, we need to embrace hierarchy. Episcopal churches are by nature hierarchical, and yet hierarchy is much disparaged in the American church. It is also true that Americans have a skewed, culturally conditioned idea of hierarchy as autocratic power over others, who have no say in what happens to them. (We are back to the matter of agency!) But not all hierarchy is exercised in this manner. Take, for example, the way business is conducted in Japan. Companies are structured in a very hierarchical manner, but when a new proposal is considered, it is common practice for the CEO to consult with everyone in the hierarchical pyramid, down to the janitor, before making a decision. By contrast, our CEOs, despite the ethos of egalitarianism, generally make the decisions first and then consult with staff to determine implementation later. In this case, the subordinates in the Japanese firm have much more agency than in the American business. So there is hierarchy and then there is hierarchy. If our churches are to remain episcopal, we are going to have to widen our understanding of what hierarchy can mean in terms of furthering God's mission.

In conclusion, I need to reiterate that this reflection is from a US perspective. Even more to the point, I have served in mainly urban areas in New York and in California, each of which have subcultures of their own. While I believe that what I have said represents the mainstream in my country, it does not adequately represent the experience of women in a minority of dioceses that were slower to accept women's ordination, or most poignantly in the three dioceses where women's ordination was not accepted till 2009. Like the Sufi parable of the blindfolded people trying to describe an elephant, I am aware that a good deal of what I have to say may apply only to my own part of God's kingdom, and may serve only for other members of the Communion to understand our situation better. And yet my fondest hope is that underneath the filters of culture, some of what I have to say will encourage and benefit women in other parts of the Communion as well, even though their contexts may be very different from mine.

6

WOMEN IN LEADERSHIP

Jane Hedges

In a recent radio interview about women being admitted to the episcopate, as the discussion moved on to the various arguments against women becoming bishops, the presenter asked me the question: 'How do you cope with this terrible frustration?' My reply was that far from being frustrated, I felt incredibly privileged to be ministering as a Canon at Westminster Abbey and that as we continue with the debate about women bishops, we need to remember that over the last 30 years the Anglican Church and even the Church of England has come an incredibly long way.

In this chapter I chart that progress, telling my own story and relating it to the experience of other women who now hold senior posts in the Church of England. I report on a recent piece of research conducted among women in stipendiary ministry and discuss the question of what particular gifts women could bring to the episcopate.

My story

Back in 1972, when I first felt called to ordination at the age of 17, I was fortunate enough to be in a parish where the priest had previously worked alongside deaconesses. So when I nervously

65

approached him saying that I believed God was calling me to be a priest I wasn't given the brush-off as many women at that time were, but rather encouraged. In fact I would go as far as to say my approach was greeted with enthusiasm! I soon came to understand that women were not at that time permitted to be priests, but at that stage I was perfectly happy with the possibility of training to be a parish worker and then hopefully becoming a deaconess. I imagined that in the years ahead I would work in a parish, assisting a vicar, and would engage mainly in pastoral work and perhaps work among children and families, and that prospect was perfectly appealing.

At the age of 20 I was recommended by ACCM (Advisory Council for the Church's Ministry) to go forward for training, which I began at St John's College Durham in 1975. By then the debate about the ordination of women to the priesthood was gaining pace and by the time I left Cranmer Hall in 1980 there was considerable disquiet and pain being experienced by women leaving college, knowing that they had completed the same training as men and in many cases had better academic qualifications, but that they were being denied the possibility of ordination.

I served my title in a team ministry in a parish that had not had a deaconess before. This was good inasmuch as I was treated as any other previous curate and was allowed by the team rector and other colleagues to gain a very wide range of experience, including being able to do as much as was legally possible liturgically. From that very positive start in parish ministry I moved on to be a team vicar, then served as a diocesan officer, followed by being appointed a residentiary canon and later a team rector, and I'm currently a Canon of Westminster.

As I look back over 30 years of ordained ministry, there have been so many wonderful moments and such a rich variety of experiences, I feel it is the most privileged role to have been called to. Coming from a background in which my early education was very poor and from a family where initially I was expected to leave school at 16, I would never have imagined in my wildest dreams that one day I would be in a position to preside at the Sung Eucharist in Westminster Abbey or preach to 2,000 people in a cathedral at the ordination of priests and deacons.

It is when I consider my own experience, together with the fact that men and women now train in equal numbers and that we have many women serving as vicars, team rectors, residentiary canons, archdeacons and deans that I realize just how much progress has been made in a relatively short time.

The experience of women now serving in senior posts

Many positive stories are told by women now serving in senior posts and these stories have a number of common threads running through them. For example, among 14 such women interviewed, all spoke of how much support and encouragement they had received, both from colleagues and their bishops. A number talked of how much they appreciated the fact that others had taken risks in believing in them and of how this had boosted their confidence and allowed them to develop their gifts and display their leadership skills. Several were appreciative of the training and mentoring they had received and of the investment of time and resources given to their ministerial development. Three people spoke of how their previous secular employment, where there was parity between men and women, had prepared them for working in a senior role within the Church. Several people had encountered what one person described as 'a thirst' for having women on the senior staff of a diocese, and a number of people described how they had been encouraged to apply for a senior post. The overwhelming feature of women's stories was the huge enjoyment and fulfilment they gained from their vocations. To quote just a few comments:

'I have been an archdeacon now for three years and love it! What is most important though is that I know that I am where God wants me to be.'

'It has been a delight to know I make a difference to people.'

67

'The ordination service speaks of stirring up the gift of God within you. I am stirred up by using those gifts and seeing them shape, challenge and encourage others to have confidence to be themselves.'

Since the mid-1990s ordained women working in UK cathedrals have met on a regular basis. Over the years this group has expanded from a handful of canons and chaplains and is now made up of two deans, 13 archdeacons and 23 residentiary canons. Known as DARC (Deans, Archdeacons and Canons), this group seeks to do the following:

- Promote mutual support for women in senior posts in the Church of England.
- Promote theological reflection on current issues, such as the nature of the Church and the nature of leadership.
- Critique current practices and offer models of good practice, for example on appointment processes.
- Offer a coherent, considered voice on issues of national church import into contemporary debates.
- Support women in ordained ministry, by offering mentoring, debriefing and guidance for vocational development.
- Monitor appointment of women to senior posts, for instance by undertaking relevant research.

In connection with the final point above, there are still relatively few women in senior posts and one reason often given for this is that many women do not wish to occupy such posts. To seek to establish if this is true I recently conducted a piece of research among the stipendiary women priests of the Church of England.

The research and the findings

The questionnaire, entitled 'Women in Senior Posts in the Church of England', was relatively simple (see Appendix 1). It

68

was distributed in October 2008 and the final return date was 10 November 2008. Around 1,600 questionnaires were sent to women on the Church Commissioners payroll. It was not sent to those who are paid by other bodies such as the National Health Service or schools and universities, and it did not go to people who had indicated to the Church Commissioners that they did not wish their details to be passed to a third party. By the cut-off date, 1,083 completed questionnaires had been returned, which I believe in itself is an indication of the interest in this issue.

Those who replied

The 1,083 were made up of women currently in the following posts: 287 curates, 210 priests-in-charge, 347 incumbents, 130 team vicars, 37 team rectors, 56 diocesan officers or chaplains, ten residentiary canons, five archdeacons and one dean.

Of all those who replied to the questionnaire, around 850 (78%) said that they would be willing to take up a senior post in the future if the opportunity arose. This seems to me to be extremely significant and runs completely counter to the argument that the reason why so few women are in se-nior posts at present is because they do not wish to take up these roles. In replying to the questionnaire people were in-vited to tick as many boxes as they wished in relation to the type of post they would be prepared to consider, and the fig-ures here indicated that women are willing to look at a wide range of possibilities: 286 indicated that they would consider being a dean; 385, an archdeacon; 439, a residentiary canon; 635, a team rector; 537, a rural dean; 288, a senior chaplain; 597, an incumbent of a major parish and 533, a diocesan director.

We must conclude from this that the majority of women in ordained ministry are confident about taking up posts that carry considerable responsibility. It is simply not true to say that wom-en do not wish to occupy senior posts.

Being a bishop?

In addition to asking about senior posts currently open to women, the question was also put: 'In the light of the recent decision by General Synod to proceed towards the consecration of women as bishops, are you open to the possibility of being called to episcopal ministry?' To this 586 women responded 'Yes', and of these 473 indicated that they would be willing to serve as either diocesan or suffragan bishops; 107 as suffragans only, and six as diocesans only.

Once again, it is quite clear that women are open to taking on this major responsibility and believe that they either already have the necessary qualities and skills to fulfil these roles or they have the potential to do so in the future.

Applying for posts

The next question posed has, for me, given a particularly significant piece of feedback. People were asked: 'What do you think would most encourage you into a senior post?' They were given the option of answering, 'An open advertisement' or 'Being requested to consider the post'.

Of the 850 who had indicated that they would be willing to take up a senior post, 680 (80%) said that they would only respond to a personal approach and only 48 (5.6%) indicated that they would respond to an open advertisement. The rest ticked the box labelled 'other' and in many instances they wrote down something along the lines of 'Being called by God'.

I believe that it is the low percentage of people willing to respond to an advertisement that may explain why relatively few women occupy senior posts at present. The Church of England has moved to a situation where many more posts are advertised and this has been seen as a positive move, offering an open approach that gives everyone the opportunity to apply for posts for which they believe they are qualified.

However, it would seem from the answers given in the questionnaire that women may be less inclined to respond to an advertisement than men. It is quite a step from indicating a general willingness to be a dean, an archdeacon or a team rector to putting oneself forward for a specific post. There is certainly some evidence to suggest that women may be more inclined than men to be put off by job descriptions and person specifications and therefore may need particular encouragement by their peers or by their bishop to recognize that they have the gifts and skills being sought.

Training needs

In the questionnaire, people were asked to indicate specific areas of training or development that would be beneficial to them in preparing for a senior role. In response, 651 people indicated that they would like training in strategic planning; 553, in management; 495, in leadership, and 415 said that they would like further theological training. A number of people also said that mentoring would be useful, and the opportunity to shadow people in senior roles; several indicated that help with interpreting finances would give them more confidence.

Women, then, are aware of areas in which they need further training in order to prepare them to take up posts with major responsibilities and which demand particular leadership skills. (A fuller analysis of the questionnaire results can be found in Appendix 2.)

Do women bring a distinctive dimension to a team or chapter?

Where women are already in senior roles it is often commented that they have brought a new dimension to them, so I would like to move on to talk about the difference it makes having a woman as part of a staff team or chapter and then apply this to what women would bring to the episcopate. Women themselves are often asked questions such as, 'So what specific difference will it make having women as bishops, or what particular gifts do you bring to this situation as a woman?'

When I am asked questions like this, I find them difficult to answer because it is hard to distinguish between what one brings to a situation as a woman as distinct from what one brings because you are you!

In a recent interview for a newspaper, when the reporter asked me just these things, I felt like saying, 'Well, it might be better to ask my male colleagues what difference it makes to them, having me as part of the chapter.' So I decided to ask a cross-section of men who have worked with women priests what difference they thought it had made to them and to the wider Church. Below are some of the responses I received.

In response to the question, 'Have you discerned any particular differences in working with a woman/women colleagues from working with men?', a man who had originally been opposed to the ordination of women but who has now worked with a woman for five years replied:

I just think it has enriched my ministry. E was ordained OLM and then became an NSM, so came out of the parish, but she has brought a whole new dimension to and a new view of how I perceive my ministry . . . I have a stipendiary curate as well and of course he and I always agree to this, that and the other and then E will say, 'Excuse me, but have you thought about X, Y and Z', and you think, 'Gosh, no we haven't and there's a lot of mileage in this.' Having her as part of our team we have complemented one another.

Another priest who, once again, was originally opposed to the ordination of women, when asked the same question, replied in this way:

In my last job I had to go to House of Bishops meetings and I was very interested in the behaviour of the bishops – I felt there was quite a lot of competition and quite a lot of powerful egos engaging with each other, sometimes relatively aggressively and sometimes competitively. It was a bit like a boys' club.

He followed this with the comment that having worked in an all-girls' school, he was not naive about girls being easy to teach! However, he went on to say about working with women:

> I do think that there is a different feel, there is not the same competitive element. This won't be true of all women, but I do think there is a sense of wanting to find a way of making things work, of engaging together, of creating an environment where people feel comfortable and come to a common mind and I think that I've encountered that with women priests.

When asked about experiencing women in leadership roles and the distinctive qualities they bring to those positions, one man commented:

> I've never worked in a team with a woman as the leader but my archdeacon is a woman. She's fantastic and I value her judgement – she's spot on and absolutely fair. I think her approach is completely different and I think it works, I think she can diffuse situations especially in a male orientated church where perhaps a male archdeacon couldn't. She just has a different way of dealing with things which is non-confrontational.

A younger man commented that he observed people relating differently to women colleagues and 'going to a deeper level' more quickly. He also said of a woman incumbent with whom he worked during his curacy, 'She was an excellent leader and much more of a natural leader than my male training incumbent. It was a very positive experience.'

However, a group of male clergy discussing the question of the distinctiveness of women within a priestly team were in agreement that it was very difficult to pin down the distinctive features a woman brought to a team apart from contributing her own particular gifts and personality. For them the important feature of

73

having a woman in a team was that the team then became representative of humanity and had a balanced feel to it and it was this feature that they thought was so important in terms of the episcopate.

Looking to the future

The title of this book is *Transfiguring Leadership* and so in this final section I try to draw out from the evidence I have gathered what women will bring to the episcopate in the Church of England, asking the question, 'Will their contribution transform it?'

It is worth reminding ourselves first about the calling of a bishop. At a service of the consecration of a bishop, before the candidate makes the declarations, the archbishop reminds the person that they are called to lead in serving and caring for the people of God, in being a chief pastor, to share in the responsibility for maintaining the unity of the Church, to uphold discipline, guard the faith, promote mission, teach, interpret the gospel, ordain new ministers, baptize, confirm and preside at the Eucharist and to have a special care for the outcast and needy. And in the prayer following the laying on of hands, the archbishop prays that the new bishop will be given humility and use their authority to heal, not to hurt, and to build up, not to destroy.

From all that has been described above, it seems to me that women are perfectly well equipped to respond to this calling.

Women, we know, are just as well trained and equipped as men to offer service and care, to interpret the gospel, to baptize and to preside at the Eucharist. From the statistics we have about women who are already in posts requiring strong leadership we also know that they are perfectly capable of upholding discipline and guarding the faith. However, from evidence and from the conversations with those who have worked with women, I believe that women bishops will have an especially strong contribution to make in terms of maintaining unity because it seems to be generally agreed that some women have a particular gift for drawing people together, for including people and finding conciliatory ways forward. Using 'authority to heal, not to hurt, to build up not to destroy' fits very well with the style of ministry that many women operate.

I leave the last word with one of the male priests interviewed who was originally opposed to the ordination of women, who says this about women bishops:

I think they would bring a new dimension. You could always argue a few years ago that they hadn't the experience of priesthood and that's fine but we are now a number of years on and we need to get on with it. I think women would bring a dimension to the House of Bishops which is sadly lacking at present.

7
SIZE MATTERS

Why Don't Women Lead Large Churches?

Kirsten Rosslyn-Smith

My experience to date has been as a curate in what could be considered a relatively large church in the UK, with an electoral roll of approx 300.

I am curious that, 18 years after the vote for women priests went through, and 16 years after the first ordinations to the priesthood, there appear to be so few women leading larger churches or being role models in this area. Why is this the case? Are there any particular barriers for women concerning larger churches? Are there internal barriers as well as external ones?

As I consider this subject I will define terms of what we may consider to be a *large* church. I look for evidence to test whether my assumption about women leading large churches is correct. Is leadership style a factor on the places women choose to minister? Are there other limiting factors? Is there a question of theological understanding on the part of some larger churches that excludes women or makes them cautious to appoint a woman?

I have undertaken a brief survey of women incumbents in the Diocese of Rochester, in southern England. Although there were very few respondents, the results show some common features about leadership in their churches.

Setting parameters

What would be considered a large church? I have used the ten largest churches in my diocese as a guideline to describe what we may consider as large. My definition from this research is based on electoral roll numbers. I have considered that a large church in this diocese is over 300 people.[1] I acknowledge that electoral roll numbers are not always the best indicator of the size of a worshipping body, and certainly there is some variation between electoral roll numbers and average weekly attendance in the ten largest churches selected.

Some figures and statistics

Figures show that in the Church of England more women are being ordained than men: for instance, in 2006, of the 478 new clergy ordained, 244 were women and 234 were men.[2] This at first glance means that slowly the numbers of male and female clergy will balance out and also that it is more likely that women will be seen in more senior posts or leading larger churches. However, the majority of the women were ordained to non-stipendiary ministry: 95 women and 128 men were ordained to full-time stipendiary ministry.[3] So there is still an imbalance in the type of ministry women are ordained into.

The fact that women outnumbered men in ordination overall, though, is interesting. Penny Jamieson, Bishop of Dunedin in New Zealand, reflects on this as she notices that fewer men are coming forward for ordination:

> I believe that it is because men assume leadership roles more naturally and more readily . . . They simply do not need the authorization of the church to exercise leadership; some built-in antennae tell them that they are always welcome, as they are.[4]

Perhaps this is reflected too in the numbers of non-stipendiary women priests. Maybe there is a need for authorization for their

77

ministry call. Yet it is noted that women often choose patterns of work that are flexible in order to fit in with other responsibilities, and non-stipendiary roles sometimes appear to offer that flexibility.[5] However, consequently fewer women will be eligible to be incumbents and trainers. It is important to note that there are some part-time stipendiary incumbents in Rochester diocese, whose roles combine the leadership status within the Church with the need for alternative patterns of ministry.

These statistics appear to correlate with the numbers of women who have part-time jobs in the country – although in March 2008 men and women held a similar number of jobs, approximately 13.6 million each. Statistics show that if there are dependants involved, then 38% of women in that category will work part-time, in contrast to 4% of men with dependants being in part-time work.[6]

It could be that this observation in the secular world is mirrored in the Church as women try to find patterns of work that fit their circumstances. Indeed, much of *Voices of This Calling*,[7] a book covering the experiences of the first generation of women priests, contains stories of women seeking to shape and work out the dual vocations of motherhood and priestly calling. They are doing this by choosing, finding and asking for creative patterns of work that would not ordinarily be available in ministry. This has the potential to bring a positive richness to the Church, as long as these are equally valued as more established patterns of ministry.[8]

In my diocese, less than half the ordained women in the diocese are in incumbencies. This, however, has to be nuanced by the associates, chaplains and those in other ministries who may have been incumbents previously.[9]

Of 61 women priests in the diocese, 25 are stipendiary incumbents, though not all are full-time; 17 are non-stipendiary, five are stipendiary curates, two are honorary curates, four are associates, one is a permanent deacon, three are chaplains; and three miscellaneous include the Director of Ministry and Training, the Spirituality Co-ordinator and the Residentiary Canon for Mission and Unity. Less than half the ordained women in the diocese are stipendiary incumbents even though they are proportionally the largest group. None of these ministers in a church with over 300 people on the electoral roll, although some curates, associates and NSMs do.[10] No ordained women work in the largest church in the diocese.

There are likely to be many different reasons why it is that fewer women are appointed to churches with larger congregations. Some will be external factors and some could be internal. For example, women are more likely to underrate their skills and experience when applying for jobs.[11]

Theological issues in larger churches

It seems to be commonly held that the majority of larger churches, not counting cathedrals, are of an evangelical theological bias.[12] Across the evangelical spectrum there are a variety of views held with regard to women in ministry, but it is now broadly more accepted. However, there can be a reluctance to appoint women so as not to offend those who are in disagreement.

In his address to a conference for larger churches,[13] Andrew Watson highlights the fact that there are fewer women clergy who would describe themselves as evangelical than not, and suggests some reasons why large, evangelical churches are failing to appoint or even attract women into ministry. He notes that many churches are able to focus on women who are 'homebuilding'[14] with children, but miss those who are building careers with or without families. This, of course, can reinforce, albeit subconsciously, gender stereotypes that can make people feel excluded. There is an issue that women are not positively encouraged into ordained ministry, even if the churches are accepting of women in ministry. Watson observes that there is 'no clear and deliberate strategy to encourage gifted women to come forward'. He cites a lack of female role models in leadership, and the problem that the only female 'leaders' that are visible in some circles or networks are the wives of leading ordained men, which further exacerbates stereotypes. In addition, when women do begin training, they find in some evangelical theological colleges a 'lack of acceptance of their ministry' – a further barrier to overcome.[15]

All of these issues are pre-ordination. Women then face further issues in their appointments from this wing of the Anglican Church. Rosie Ward reports one case of an 'able and experienced woman priest' who applied to be vicar of a large evangelical church. 'Although she was told after the interview that she was the best candidate, the interviewers said that they could not bring themselves to appoint her.'[16]

Is there perhaps a lack of imagination and a feeling of risk in appointing women? While strong theological standpoints can be respected and may take time to change, it is hard to accept lack of opportunity in the form of unprovable discrimination from churches who say they do accept women's ministry.

Interestingly, the majority of women end up in smaller parishes.[17] Yet church growth figures show that the churches led by a female incumbent are much more likely to grow than those with a male incumbent.[18] So it might be that many small and rural parishes are beginning to grow under the leadership of women. We could look at this in two ways: that women *choose* smaller parishes and are good at making them grow, or that is just where they happen to end up and they simply fulfil their call in that place. Either way it seems that size is essentially not an issue for women. It is more a question of where their skills and abilities can be used and valued.[19]

Internal factors

Throughout the Church there is the desire on the part of many to see women in senior posts, not just in episcopal ministry but in parishes of all sizes. While there is more that could be done to encourage this, there can be reluctance on the part of women to step up for more senior posts. Why is this?

An article with the title, 'My Glass Ceiling is Self-Imposed',[20] written by a senior female executive in Canada, sheds some light on this. The author describes how her company positively encourages women in flexibility of working hours and provision of various facilities, such as dry cleaning. Yet when she was offered a promotion that would have 'made' her, she turned it down. Why? Because her family were happy where they lived, her husband was happy in his job, grandparents were nearby and their quality of life was good. She had no desire to disrupt this.

Perhaps in this we can see a propensity for women to take a much wider or 'familiarcentric' view of the options they are presented with, and so to tailor their work around the survival or flourishing of their family. The article finishes with two thoughts: 'It is an ongoing battle that many women face – the balance between career and family and how ultimately we are able to manage both in the end.' Acknowledging the work to break 'glass ceilings', she also wants to recognize that 'not all females are willing to give up what it might take to get there'.[21]

Although maternity and how each family chooses to structure itself inevitably places practical and emotional limits on what is possible and desirable for women to take on, this is only one barrier that is faced. Leadership roles can also be made harder when they clash with external 'preconceptions, stereotypes and expectations' of others, relating to such issues.[22] The different perceptions of men and women in family situations mean that the same action could be interpreted positively for men but negatively for women because it runs contrary to expectation.

Visibility and biblical models of women's leadership

It is interesting that the members of a small group of women priests, when asked about biblical leadership models, all gave male leadership figures as examples, except for one, who chose Mary Magdalene. The others chose Gideon, Moses and Paul.

It strikes me that, first, visibility of women in any leadership role in the Bible is not high, although they are present. Leadership in most cases is male. We tend to draw on these and use them as examples in a genderless fashion, identifying with the stories of the people. It emerged in questioning of the group that

81

the leaders who found it hard to accept their call, such as Gideon and Moses, were identified with. They as characters had humility towards God, but a less than healthy self-esteem. It is perhaps telling that the women should choose these.

As I reflected personally on this I realized that there is not much possibility of choosing women as examples in such roles because with many of the women who we can quote as leaders, such as Phoebe, Priscilla and the recently uncovered Junia the apostle, there is little information to identify with. The fact that they are mentioned at all is powerful testimony to their leadership in a patriarchal and unaccepting cultural climate. It demonstrates that women took on such roles in the early Church. Any further information about them or the way they executed their ministry is scarce.

There are, however, examples of women taking the lead in different ways in the Old Testament. In *Leading Ladies*, Jeanne Porter uses women from the Old Testament as possible paradigms for different forms of women's leadership. She considers the midwives in Exodus, Miriam the choreographer and prophetic leader, Esther as intercessor and Deborah as weaver of relationships.[23] While this is illuminating and helpful, and one can identify with the ways in which these women had influence and led, it requires exegesis and imagination to see this. Yet they stand out against a backdrop of patriarchal religion that gave little power to women.[24] They are the extraordinary ones used by God in the salvation story of his people. These women are often sidelined, neither credited for their leadership nor easily seen.[25]

However, it is highly significant how women appear in the Gospels and the manner in which they are treated by Jesus. Their contribution, presence and witness are vital and this must have been the case, otherwise they could easily have been written or edited out. Consider how radical it was for Mary, Martha's sister, to be sitting at the feet of the rabbi, having chosen the better part;[26] the way in which the resurrection is revealed to the women in the Gospels and the Lord himself revealing himself to Mary before the others; or the women who were written or rather translated away by collective nouns given only masculine form. Visibility is a problem; they are not seen in the same way as the men were. Yet we find that there are few details about some of the male disciples and followers of Christ. We can tell more of the life and response of the unnamed woman at the well, from John 4, than we can of Bartholomew.

Leadership styles

Whenever leadership style is discussed there can be a reticence to identify specifically a woman's way of leading. Men and women will have a variety of styles, some learned and some natural to them; making generalizations can be counter-productive. However, all the women who answered the survey cited collaborative style as their preference. This seems to be borne out in the literature on this subject. Rosie Ward cites research in 1997 from the Christian Research Association, which 'found that male clergy were more likely to be "directors" than women clergy who were primarily team people'.[27]

In the few replies to the survey I received, there was a discrepancy between the natural models of leadership that women incumbents would choose to operate and the expectations of their parishioners.[28] All said they were collaborative and wanted to build teams to work with and alongside others. In terms of biblical models, one used the body of Christ as an image.[29] Some find, however, that in their contexts a collaborative form of leadership is not an accepted mode of operation. One incumbent notes:

> I feel pushed into giving a stronger lead than I would want to do, standing firm and speaking my mind in a tougher way than I would naturally choose. A more gentle, conciliatory style of leadership, even 'Servant Leadership' in the way that many would describe it, is not an option here . . . I'd be ground into the dust![30]

Another states: 'although it's not my ideal, leadership here is mostly from the front. Biblical model? I really feel for Moses!'[31]

83

Carol Becker comments on the situation in the United States with what seems to be a pattern emerging from research that women are seemingly placed in churches that are smaller, not necessarily of their own choice:

> Once in the system, clergywomen's ability to move up is hampered and they continue to be called to smaller, less secure congregations in some denominations . . . Once in the parish there is growing evidence that clergywomen are accepted by the parishioners; nevertheless, very recent studies confirm the particular difficulty clergywomen have in moving to senior pastorates.[32]

It seems that there is a perceived element of risk in women leading large churches. So is there something in the way women lead that makes them more likely to go to minister in churches that are smaller?

Evidence does not appear to support this. Ironically it seems that smaller churches are more likely to be reliant on clergy rather than be looking for a greater level of lay participation, hence the battle faced by those surveyed in building teams.

Conclusion

So do women lead large churches? In October 2008, the Revd Rosalyn Murphy was licensed priest-in-charge of St Thomas', Blackburn, in the north of England. With combined congregational figures of over 550 people this makes it the largest evangelical, charismatic church in the town.[33] As women are beginning to be appointed to large churches, this will hopefully inspire others.

There are various reasons for the lack of women leading large churches. Some issues are theological and there can be continued unease, particularly in the evangelical wing of the Church, about appointing women. Family can be an issue: caring for children or elderly parents, while also dealing with others' preconceptions and expectations. This may, however, lead women to seek creative patterns of ministry that could benefit many and enrich the church's ministry. It could also prevent them from taking on particular posts – which may say as much about the post as about the person. The ways in which women lead are diverse, but there seems to be a common collaborative strand which is, perhaps ironically, something much sought after particularly in larger churches seeking new incumbents.[34]

From my survey, which is admittedly a small sample, for these women in ministry the main criterion is a sense of call to the place they end up in[35] – size doesn't matter.

Much of the work in this area focuses on statistics or personal story and anecdote. Story is certainly a particularly feminine mode of expression, and perhaps voicing stories can precipitate change at some level.

This chapter merely scratches the surface of this subject area, and there are many facets that would benefit from further research. It would also be good to expand the research to explore a wider picture, mapping where women minister and why, or compare some dioceses according to their support of women's ministry by their bishops. This question for me came out of my own curiosity over not seeing women leading larger churches, and personal ease or unease about large congregations. I am indebted to the work and encouragement of Rosie Ward at CPAS whose research and analysis in this field is invaluable.

8

WOMEN AND LEADERSHIP

What's the Difference?[1]

Jane Shaw

The transformation of leadership requires more than the admission of the excluded and marginalized, even though that step is absolutely essential for the Church to be true to its own Christian anthropology – namely, that to be human is to be radically equal one to another and radically alive – and thus to the development of new models of leadership. However, I suggest in this chapter that the mere admission of the marginalized into the power structures will not necessarily change things, but it will raise questions about how we lead, what the Church is, and how we create community.

Gendered perceptions of leadership

Leadership in contemporary life brings particular difficulties and pressures for both men and women. Public figures are the repository for our projected fears and hopes: we make them what we need and want them to be. The hazards of public life affect those in leadership positions in the Church, as any priest or minister or prominent lay leader knows, and they especially have an impact on the life of bishops: as James Woodward

86

has written, 'Bishops are a focus of all kinds of fantasy and displacement.'[2]

Women in leadership positions embody the broader social revolution we are going through. They are icons of the shift, in the last few decades, that has led to the re-making of our private and public worlds. When women step into the public world, they necessarily raise questions about our priorities as a society. At what price will anyone (male or female, old or young, parent or not) endure public life? Why is the quality of political leadership often so poor, and what can we do to attract more able and talented people into such positions? How do we balance family, friendship commitments and work? What are our priorities as individuals?

These issues especially come up when women enter the public sphere, for at least two reasons. First, those who come from outside the establishment see it differently: those from the margins almost always have a fresh perspective on the mainstream. So women themselves have raised some of these questions on entering a culture from which they were for so long excluded. This makes their perspective important and challenging. Second, whenever a new thing happens people can react with fear or hope. For those whose response is fear, the instinctual reaction is to lash out at those who represent what is challenging them. For those whose response is hope, their first instinct might be right-sized support, but it could equally well be to load a set of unreasonable expectations onto those who embody their hopes for the future. Women in leadership can, then, be caught between these attacks and expectations, with little room to be themselves.

We face these questions in the Church no less than we do in society, perhaps more acutely. Christianity has always had a paradoxical attitude to women. On the one hand, its anthropology teaches that women and men are both made in the image and likeness of God; its theology of salvation says that women and men are equally recipients of grace. On the other hand, some Pauline injunctions suggest that women's activities should be limited, and such texts have frequently been used to curtail what women can do to such an extent that women are seen as

87

inferior human beings whose gifts are given less value in the pub-lic world of the Church than the gifts of men. This paradox has been worked out again and again in Christian history. Paul him-self embodied it, happily working alongside women most of the time – think of the list of female co-workers in his greeting to the church at Rome – but when the going got tough, as at Corinth, his anxiety got the better of him and, as he attempted to advise an unruly church on how to behave, women became the recipi-ents of his criticisms. Revival movements, such as the Quakers in the mid-seventeenth century and the Methodists in the eight-eenth century, often encouraged the participation of women in their early days: Quaker women prophesied and Methodist women preached. But when those movements began to get insti-tutionalized, to go from sect to church in the sociological sense, to seek respectability, they eradicated women's leadership and marginalized their contributions. Throughout Christian history women, their gifts and their capacity for leadership have been sacrificed in the face of fear and in the resulting desire to retain the status quo.

It is no surprise that we find ourselves facing the consequences and tensions of this paradoxical attitude towards women in our own day. Katharine Jefferts Schori, the Presiding Bishop of the Episcopal Church, has certainly been the screen upon which a number of conservative figures in the Anglican Communion have played out their fantasies and fears. As the Communion fights about the issue of homosexuality, Jefferts Schori – as an American, female leader – has been on the receiving end not only of prejudicial remarks about women (especially from branches of the Communion and parts of the Episcopal Church itself that have no sense of the value of women's leadership) but also of a certain hysteria about homosexuality, directed against the Episcopal Church because it elected and consecrated a gay man in a same-sex partnership. Go on some of the conservative Angli-can websites and you will find some truly appalling blogs about this woman; irrational hatreds are placed at the doorstep of the duly elected female Presiding Bishop. Jefferts Schori has herself articulated what is at the heart of this issue: 'While the current controversy has much to do with varying understandings of scriptural authority, there is also an element that has to do with a changing understanding of who may exercise authority.'[3]

Symbolism is complex (which is to say that symbols are multivalent): but while recognizing that much that is negative can be projected onto iconic figures, and conversely that we often project unrealistic expectations onto those same icons, we should not underestimate the symbolic importance of seeing 'someone like us' by the altar, exercising authority, taking decisions, leading the church. All the female bishops testify to the number of times women come up to them and say how important it is for them to see 'someone like them' in the highest offices of the Church. As the first female bishop of the Anglican Communion, Bishop Barbara Harris, puts it of her own work as suffragan bishop of Massachusetts, 'Women and girls were encouraged to feel that they truly had a place in the Church and people of colour expressed their pride and their joy in God's doing "a new thing".'[4]

Exercising leadership

Just as the entry of women into public life has raised questions more broadly in our society about what our values and priorities are as individuals, families and communities, so as women have assumed roles of leadership in various organizations, including the Church, we have been prompted to ask what models of leadership we want, and ultimately what community and church mean to us and what we want them to be.

Some people have presumed or expected that once women entered the priesthood and once they became a part of the hierarchy of the Church – whether as priests or laity – then the institutional Church would magically become a better place. Hierarchies would be flattened; teamwork would be the norm. I do not share this presumption, primarily because it usually rides on the back of gendered presuppositions about women being more 'naturally' pastoral, less competitive and more empathetic and collaborative. Some women have those characteristics; so do some men. The point is not about what women 'naturally' are, as if we could ever know that – in the last few decades we have come to articulate powerfully the ways in which culture shapes what we understand women and men to be – but rather, as noted earlier, that those who come into the centre of power from the margins and a history of exclusion can often see it differently, with fresh eyes. And this may indeed lead us to new models of leadership – though not necessarily.

Once someone is given access to the centre, once he or she is given power, then they may simply reproduce the same patterns of hierarchical leadership and, what's more, draw up the ladder behind them, or at the very least insist that others in their wake endure the same miserable experience to get to where they are. I call this the 'cleaning lavatories through Yale' syndrome, based on a conversation I had many years ago with one of my professors at Harvard who said that as he had cleaned bathrooms to finance his education through Yale, so I should do the same through Harvard. Just admitting women to the episcopate, for example, will not *necessarily* make the episcopate a more humane or egalitarian institution. Indeed, it is often easier to analyse an institution's structures, and especially its faults, from the outside, or when first entering it. The more comfortable we get with the whole thing then the more we may want to fit in, the less we may want to rock the boat and, ultimately, the more we will 'see through a glass darkly'.

As noted earlier, the transformation of leadership therefore requires more than the admission of the excluded and marginalized, even though the Church is called to do that in order to be true to its own theology of human nature. The marginalization of certain categories of human being by the Church means that as Christians we fall short of Christian teaching about the nature of humanity all the time. While recognizing that there is always a tension between the ideal and the institutional, between the 'now' and the 'not yet' (the latter a theological tension as we move with longing towards the kingdom of heaven on earth), it must be the Christian teaching about personhood that shapes our models of leadership. Indeed, one of the tasks of any leader is to hold that larger vision of what might be, and understand what the reality is in relation to it; to assess how what we are actually doing measures up to the ideal; and to know what changes need to happen in order to grow closer to that 'not yet' but yearned for.

I now want to discuss two factors that are important for the transformation of leadership – which will in turn affect the transformation of our churches, our local communities and our society. The first factor is the basis on which we appoint and elect leaders; the second is the discernment of the patterns of leadership we want – and being intentional about their implementation.

How are we to elect and appoint leaders? Until quite recently in the Church of England, the way someone learned that they had been appointed dean of a cathedral, bishop of a particular diocese or canon of a 'plum' cathedral, was that a rather ordinary brown envelope dropped through the letter box. Inside that was a thick white envelope with 10 Downing Street embossed in black on the back. The late Henry Chadwick used to tell the amusing story of how, when he became Dean of Christ Church, Oxford in 1969, he received the Downing Street letter:

I was lecturing on a Swan Hellenic Cruise which took us to Greece. At Nauplion on the quay there stood a vast black car, the Maltese driver of which announced that he had a strictly confidential letter for Professor Chadwick, in an enormous white envelope, and was instructed to wait for an answer to be taken back to the Ambassador in Athens. So I had to go shopping for paper in Nauplion![5]

In this system, the appointee was always at the receiving end; a gift was dropped from a great height and one was to be grateful. This form of appointment therefore created a culture of dependency. In the UK we are now moving ourselves out of this pattern, and focusing on selection through application, discernment, gifts and experience. In all of this, perhaps the thing we are least used to doing is assessing our gifts in relationship to the

91

post or task at hand. The old system was (at least until the last few years) shrouded in secrecy, so a person was never encouraged to think about their gifts or what post they might be especially suited to fill. And yet for women that assessment of gifts is especially vital. Too often presuppositions about 'what women can do' get in the way of fair appointments – and of course this unfairness has been institutionalized in the Church of England in that it is exempt from sex discrimination legislation – and so it is on gifts that we must focus. It is on the basis of a person's gifts (not their gender or age or sexual orientation or ethnicity or any other similar factor) that they must be appointed to positions of responsibility and authority.

On the one side we have gifts; on the other, we need blueprints for the type of leadership we want. The two are related. Many of the earliest churches, in the first couple of centuries, tried to function according to 'gifts', and this often meant that their orders of ministry were far more than the eventually institutionalized three (eight at the church in Rome, for example). There is inscriptional, archaeological evidence that women in early Christianity were presbyters and that they exercised oversight as bishops – but just as important, they were also martyrs, teachers, prophets, widows and deacons, exercising their gifts (alongside men) accordingly in the local community.[6] This emphasis on multiple leaders in varying areas according to their gifts enables the 'flattening out' of ministry and leadership; the emphasis then tends to lie on the relational rather than the hierarchical. This means that the person (or persons) 'at the top' (the vicar, the bishop) is constantly giving away responsibility *with* authority; and that is the key thing – that responsibility comes with authority (too often in church life we give people responsibility but no authority, which is miserable for everyone). This develops, ideally, into shared leadership. Some dioceses, especially in the Episcopal Church in the USA, are beginning to talk about shared episcope.

At the heart of this form of leadership is the notion of the gift: that the more one gives away, the more abundance there is.[7] The more that people are given tasks and responsibility with authority and the more leadership is shared, then the more the church grows, the more the community flourishes, the more people want to participate. Jesus emphasizes this over and over again in the Gospels, most obviously in the feeding of the thousands. Leadership in this model will come to emphasize community and relationships – both inside and outside the Church – rather than shoring up the institution and 'keeping the show on the road'. As churches and other emerging religious communities move towards this form of ministry and leadership, so they will be mirroring a development in the business world. This non-hierarchical and less centralized form of leadership and power is most obvious in the success of the internet, but it can be seen in other organizations too, where the absence of centrally located and locatable leaders has actually enabled rather than hampered growth and development.[8]

None of this should stop us doing what we do with authority; in fact, that is always going to be central to leadership, whoever exercises it and however they exercise it. In order for a community to flourish, in order for people to feel welcome – comfortable with putting their toes into the water of faith, for example – the authority that comes with leadership needs to be exercised with confidence and ease.

What does any of this have to do with gender? The entry of women into leadership roles has prompted us to reflect on what leadership is and might be in the churches. This has pointed to the tension with which we live: that the gospel teaches that all are made in the image and likeness of God, all are radically equal, all therefore have gifts to offer, but the reality is that too few have the opportunity to exercise these gifts, and our leadership models do not necessarily encourage it. It is therefore incumbent upon us as Christians to enable and encourage all to exercise their gifts, to flourish as women and men made in the image of God. In the 'not yet', in the kingdom for which we strive, this has nothing to do with gender. But in our fallen world, with our obsession with sexual difference and all the other differences that divide us as human beings, we keep having to return to the most basic of theological premises – about what it means as Christians to be human, and what that means for each of us to flourish.

PART 3

FACING THE CHANGE

9
BENEDICT REVISITED

Rosalind Brown

I live, work and worship in Durham Cathedral, a building that by its very presence reminds me daily of the psalmist's experience: 'Lord, you have been our dwelling place through every generation.' The cathedral stands, rooted, strong and welcoming, giving little away about the millennium of turbulent history that has happened within and around it. It has survived wars, famines, traumas and disasters, including the dissolution of the monasteries, the Reformation and the Commonwealth period when it was desecrated and used as a prison. It has survived not just as a building but as a living, worshipping community that continues to bear witness to the gospel in the north-east of England. It is unique among cathedrals in the way it is owned by the local people; whatever their faith, Durham Cathedral is their cathedral, their history, the place they call home.

During the 1990s I lived in the United States and experienced dislocation from my history and tradition. I had to come away from the familiar to understand how formative it was for me. I lived for most of that time in a Benedictine community of men and women in a former steel town in the Rust Belt. Returning to the UK and moving eventually to Durham has brought various strands together for me in new ways in an English cathedral where 450 years of monasticism still echo among us. Benedict did not intend to establish an institution but provided a school

97

of the Lord's service[1] which enables us to respond to God and mature in our discipleship, and that is as true today in Durham as it was when there were monks here.

As I have reflected on the 2008 Episcope conference, and the ongoing moves to find a way forward that embodies fully the ministry of women but also respects people who do not see this as an appropriate development in the tradition, I wonder if Benedict's insights – writing as he was for people who held a common commitment but nevertheless did not always agree with each other[2] – have something to say to all of us, not about the issue itself but about how we can live graciously and faithfully with the demands and questions it places on us. Benedict gave his monks the sometimes awkward gift of each other and then helped them to appropriate it. He concludes his Rule with chapters that remind us of the link between the way we relate to one another and our way to God, and urges respect, tolerance and concern for the good of others.[3] It may be helpful to hear afresh from Benedict that this is a good and godly way but that it places responsibilities on all of us to seek the common good.[4] There is not space here to explore how specific insights from a monastic community relate to our different context, but the principles underlying the vows are a place to start. His three vows of stability, obedience and conversion of life offer a framework for that daily maturing to which we are all called because we hold a common commitment to God though our baptism, whatever our views on the ordination of women.

Stability is not the same as stagnation. I find Michael Casey's definition of stability, honed by his years of monastic living, as what it takes to stay upright on a surf-board, very evocative and helpful.[5] Other ways to think of this include the stability needed to ride a bicycle, a plant being rooted so it can grow, or the stability of a home that facilitates a child's healthy development. In all cases, there is a dynamic context; momentum is involved. It is not about vegetating, resisting change or upholding the status quo, but keeping our balance on the move. Casey is Australian and obviously has the rolling waves of Australian beaches in mind as well as the skill of surfers in bending, stretching, shifting their weight and their direction in order to move with the waves and experience the exhilaration of surfing. Life in God's world is exhilarating and challenging and, unless we are prepared to bend and stretch, to work to maintain our balance, we will fall off the surfboard. It's a vivid way to describe discipleship.

Stability means staying with and in a situation (Benedictine monks do not have the option of moving to another monastery when things get uncomfortable) and being committed to each other while we work through the differences. It means that we forgo the option of rendering others powerless by withdrawing in the face of problems; something easier said than done. The Benedictine way recognizes that this is the community in which I am set; I may not like it all the time but I am committed to it and we will work things through. Artists know that there is no freedom without limitations, and stability means that we accept the limitations of our situation and seek to follow God in the midst of it. If we can't find and be found by God where we are, it won't happen somewhere else.

Then there is the second vow, obedience. Our example here is Christ, who learned obedience through what he suffered.[6] Those are strong words: obedience is learned, it does not come easily but requires dedication and attention and we should not be surprised if we suffer in the process of learning it. Obedience asks us where our ultimate allegiance lies so that in facing immediate questions we do not lose sight of our foundational commitment to follow Christ, whatever the cost. Obedience requires humility and is responsive; it involves discernment so that we don't simply yield to the voice that shouts loudest or longest, but discern wisely before making choices. The Rule of Benedict begins with the instruction 'listen', because God is always speaking a fresh word since, as the scriptures remind us, God is always doing new things that require us to adjust. Listening brings with it action since the Bible implies that we haven't listened if we don't act; obedience expresses our love in action and is courageous and intelligent. In monastic communities, leaders are to listen not only to long-standing members but also to the youngest and newest member who might have insights others have overlooked – an insight in itself that we often overlook.[7] And in turn the members of the community promise obedience without murmur or delay, respecting one another as they acknowledge each other's weaknesses. Benedict expects holiness to be forged through rubbing shoulders with those with whom we disagree, because they are the people who will knock off our rough edges. Obedience keeps us chaste in our relationships so that we don't use or manipulate others for our own ends but can sustain mature and holy relationships, shown, in part, in the way we handle disagreements. Vignettes from Durham Cathedral suggest that the monks knew all about this: fellowship was robust at times!

The third vow is conversion of life, the other side of the coin to stability. Benedict wanted all the monks to become more and more conformed to Christ, more Christ-like. This conversion of life cannot happen without change, sometimes dramatic, sometimes imperceptible and only seen in retrospect when we realize how far we have come. For we are pilgrims, always travelling with and towards God who is always doing a new thing, opening up new possibilities in situations that seemed locked into a cycle of death, reminding us that the tomb is empty and he is not here, he is risen. Conversion of life may mean letting go so that our hands are open and empty to receive God's new gifts. To do that we can't have too tight a grip on people and situations and may need to ask ourselves what would be the hardest thing that God could ask us to allow to be changed. We are created in the image of a creative God and our creativity is an aspect of conversion of life, enabling us to work with what we have, not what we wish we had, to make something that might have looked impossible from the raw materials to hand. Dare we risk the invitation to let go of our control and let God take the lead in our lives as a dance partner does? Stability and conversion of life allow us to move gracefully with God as our partner on the dance floor of life.

These Benedictine vows were lived for centuries in the buildings I now walk around day by day. They sustained and challenged people through times of immense upheaval and trials in the Church and nation which make our situation look placid in comparison. The ultimate trial came on the last day of 1539 when, thanks to the edict of the king that ruled unilaterally that the church's polity was changed, Prior Hugh Whitehead led the monks into the cathedral to recite Compline, as they had done for centuries. When the last notes of plainchant died away, the monks processed out of the cathedral for the very last time. Centuries of tradition died at that moment. There was no going back; everything they knew, everything they had taken as a given, was ended at a stroke and their task was now to carve out something new. And the records hint that what sustained them as they made the transition to being a dean and chapter was their monastic vows that freed them to face the new way of life. Their stability was grounded in their worship,[8] their obedience was expressed in their acceptance of the changes and their continued commitment to one another,[9] and their conversion of life is shown in their discovery of new ways of being the community of Durham Cathedral – living separately, offering hospitality (still central to their life) as individuals rather than as a community, marrying and having families. Geoffrey Moorhouse captures the cost of this transition vividly:

> How much this novel corporation of Anglican clergymen missed the company of those of their old brethren who had been pensioned off in the world outside, with whom they had lived (in some cases for decades) closely, we have no means of knowing, but the lack of general intercourse in the refectory and frater, the regularity with which all had gathered in the cemetery to remember those who had gone before, must have impinged upon all of them, quite painfully for some.[10]

Here was the ultimate conflict of opinion on what it meant to be the Church; centuries of tradition were swept away for people who knew no other way to be faithful to God. Walter Brueggemann refers to psalms of 'orientation', 'disorientation' and 'reorientation'[11] and, as they recited those psalms daily, the years after 1539 must have felt like the definitive experience of disorientation. And yet Durham Cathedral is here today; the cathedral community worships together at least three times a day, we work together, we inhabit the same spaces as the monks did, we offer hospitality and we are recovering actively the Benedictine tradition as a guide to life.[12] Some of our life would be familiar to the last monks, much would require their adjustment, but the tradition has not only survived the disorientation, it has grown. The reorientation began and has continued through stability, obedience and conversion of life. As I write, discussions about the way forward for episcopacy continue and it is stability, obedience and conversion of life that can help us as a Church.

Once, when visiting a National Trust property, I discovered as I walked clockwise round the extensive grounds that whoever did the signage expected everyone to walk in an anticlockwise direction. I saw several signs with arrows on but none of them told me which way to go. Instead they all pointed back the way I had come, confirming that I had come from the right direction but leaving me to make my own decisions about where to go at junctions. Hebrews tells us, 'Faith is the assurance of things hoped for, the conviction of things not seen. By faith Abraham obeyed when he was called to set out not knowing where he was going.'[13] In other words, he only found out as he went along that he was going the right way. Otherwise there would have been no faith involved, just the spiritual equivalent of following directional arrows, which is easier but not an act of faith. The whole biblical story tells us that God has made us for more than following directional arrows: we are clockwise walkers. That's partly why the Bible paints such a messy picture and tells stories of humans trying to be faithful, not of robots doing what they are programmed to do. In the play *A Man for All Seasons*, Thomas More, facing the likelihood of death, says, 'God made . . . man . . . to serve him wittily, in the tangle of his mind.'[14] We are called to intelligent, thoughtful, faithful, witty discipleship, not to robotic compliance. So perhaps we should not be too dismayed that it is taking us a while to untangle the implications of women in the episcopate; it is part of faithful discipleship in a Church that has become used to one way of living and is moving towards another. Obedience requires us to keep going bravely, walking by faith not by sight through what may feel like a period of disorientation when there is no going back, only arrows telling us we have come the right way. All we know is that when the time of reorientation does come it will be different from how things were because we have all been changed by the experience and will have new and deepened understandings of episcopacy.

My experience of living in two nations famously described as being divided by a common language taught me that it is the common language that can make it so hard to deal with times when what looks and sounds familiar has taken on a wholly different meaning. You don't have to learn a new word for something (to say it in another language), you have to learn to live with a new or nuanced meaning to a familiar and trusted word. There is not the option to retain its old meaning in new circumstances.[15] Only those who have struggled with letting go of inherited meanings can grasp what that can do to the soul – it feels like part of what has formed you is being asked of you in order to live in a new situation that is disarmingly and hauntingly familiar as well as relentlessly different. I was surprised how much I wanted Americans to understand what words meant to me and what letting go of traditional British meanings cost me in terms of who I am. At times it seems easier to look for a third way unrelated to the other two – to learn the word in French – rather than learn new shades of meaning to a familiar word that demand something of us. The challenge of stability and conversion of life is not to deny the validity of the meanings we bring to anything from the past but, like a poet rather than a translator, to grow from one meaning to greater depth of meaning rather than use a replacement foreign word or stop speaking altogether.

I wonder whether this is part of our struggle as a Church facing the questions raised by women in the episcopate? We know what the word means from our experience; it is deeply and profoundly a part of us and for two millennia a male episcopate is all that has been modelled to us. When I moved to Durham as the first female canon residentiary, one of the choristers was perplexed and his mother reported a conversation along the lines of, 'But Canon Brown can't be a Canon.' 'Why not?' 'Because there's no one to show her how to do it.' The rationale for this was simple: in the choir (which now has a girls' top line but then was only boys) younger choristers are mentored by older choristers and in an all-male environment it was tacitly assumed that gender was significant. The fact that a woman might bring gifts that enrich the cathedral and create new ways to be a canon had not entered this chorister's thinking because until now he had no need to think this way. Three years later, when I returned from a sabbatical, several people spoke of their gladness that the procession into Evensong was again no longer entirely masculine: what had once been quite normal had become uncomfortable because a new meaning for the familiar had been learned. I suggest that the Church faces the challenge of learning to understand and inhabit the word 'episcopate' in its profounder meanings rather than shouting louder in the language we know.

If Brueggemann gives us a framework for thinking of the situation we find ourselves in as a Church, the Benedictine vows offer us a way to live in it faithfully. Benedict placed hospitality at the heart of monastic living, and all guests are to be received as though they are Christ. That requires a creative tension between the order given by tradition and routine in life and the disruption caused by guests. Benedict seems to want just enough chaos to stop the order getting suffocating or inhibiting because, as Joan Chittister writes, 'The message to the stranger is clear: Come right in and disturb our perfect lives. You are the Christ for us today.'[16] Jesus dealt with interruptions throughout his ministry and gives us his own example of hospitality: when two of John's disciples asked him where he was staying he simply invited them to 'come and see'.[17] Benedict invites us to risk being hospitable to people who herald change in our lives, to invite them in and risk not knowing when or how reorientation will occur. We can be sustained as we do this, as were the monks in Durham in 1539, by Benedict's wisdom.

As we see signs that tell us we have come in the right direction on our pilgrimage and anticipate further developments towards an episcopate of both men and women in the Church of England, our underlying calling to become more faithful disciples committed to each other's maturity in Christ is paramount. That is what

Benedict facilitated for his monks, and he knew that this concerned not just people's actions but the motivation behind them: the reshaping of lives from within. As I kneel in my cathedral stall, knowing that I am the first woman to do so, and pray for those for whom this is a disorientating time, I take encouragement from my forebears here at Durham who, in their disorientation, were challenged to find completely new ways to express their commitment to God and were launched out on a journey of faith. To mix metaphors, when all the directional arrows only pointed backwards to where they had come from, they rode the waves rolling around them. Their Benedictine heritage saw them through the transition and gave us Durham Cathedral as we know it today. It can do the same for us. For all of us, there is hope in Benedict's little phrase, 'never despair of the mercy of God'.[18]

10

IN SEARCH OF A SPIRITUALITY OF AUTHORITY

Jenny Gaffin

I have long been enthralled by Antoine de Saint-Exupéry's children's classic *The Little Prince*.[1] This book has been a source of inspiration, exasperation and courage for me as I have travelled the somewhat implausible journey from lay work in London, in Soho's gay scene, through to a curacy in a wonderfully blessed Anglo-Catholic parish in Poole, on the south coast of England. Told by an old man disillusioned with the rationality that dominates adult life, *The Little Prince* contains within its disarmingly simple poetic form an extraordinary depth of theological wisdom on the nature of relationships and love, and such a powerful insight into the spirituality of authority that it bears examination in the context of the Church.

The Little Prince lives alone on a remote planet until completely by chance a seed, flying through space, takes root in his soil. Having satisfied himself that it is neither a tree whose roots will destroy the whole planet nor a common weed, he welcomes it. He waters it and puts it under a screen to protect it from the cold, until it grows into a beautiful but terribly prickly flower, who proceeds to take over his life. In despair, he leaves her behind, travelling from planet to planet, encountering all manner of human folly, until on earth he finally learns how to love, and is able to return to care for his flower.

As a child, this story released my imagination and engaged my heart. I spent hours staring out of my window at the night sky, wondering at its hidden mysteries and straining to hear the laughter of the Little Prince ringing out from his planet. Somewhere out there was an alcoholic drinking to forget his drunkenness; somewhere was a geographer self-satisfied with his academic talent; and somewhere was a flower, nurtured and cherished. When as an adult at the beginning of my career I was blown well outside my familiar world into the heart of Soho, the parallels between the flower's reception and my own did not escape me. To say that it was an unusual place for a heterosexual, teetotal, newly committed Christian to take root is something of an understatement, and indeed the other members of staff were initially as bemused as I was. They checked me over thoroughly to ensure that this innocent-looking seedling wasn't about to damage their planet – no, I wasn't going to denounce them for seeking healthy ways to express their sexuality; no, I wasn't in denial about my own sexual orientation; no, I wasn't afraid of mixing with the Buddhists, Muslims, self-proclaimed experts in angels and feng-shui practitioners who populated their world. And yes, amazingly enough, I was feeling more than a little vulnerable as I landed in their midst and looked about me. And yet, despite the disorientation, there was a spark of joy. Gazing out of the window as a child, long before the Christian language of love and resurrection featured on my radar, I had known with absolute certainty that somewhere out there, veiled in darkness and against all the odds, there was hidden beauty, and it had given me hope. As I looked round me at Soho's bewildering landscape, newly theologically equipped, I was equally convinced that God's deepest beauty was embedded in the heart of this community. My task was to find a way of using such authority as I had to enable it to flourish.

I sought inspiration in the figure of a king encountered by the Little Prince as he first travels through space. To all outward appearances, this king is an absolute monarch. There is no confusion of roles in his presence: he rules strictly and he tolerates no disobedience. All are his subjects – the other stars, all visitors to his planet, and the single other inhabitant of the planet, a long-suffering rat, over whom he reigns in majesty. Yet for all the show of power, the king's authority is not as straightforwardly autocratic as it seems, as the rat by now has learned. The rat knows that to the king, he is an errant subject. But he also knows that the king needs him, and that having condemned him to death yet once more this proudest of monarchs will eventually be merciful and pardon him. And so, despite appearances to the contrary, the planet is in fact run according to a benign 'win-win' arrangement: the rat misbehaves once in a while, knowing that he will keep his life, and in return the king has a chance to demonstrate his power and exercise his magnanimity. All is well and all is reasonable, to misquote Mother Julian, and the king prides himself on the rationality of his authority.

There is much that is strong and wise in the king. As anyone who has ever managed volunteers knows only too well, authority rests not on the ability to have your own way all the time, but on the ability to modify your decisions according to what is possible given the rapidly changing forces of personality and circumstance at work around you. This is particularly the case somewhere as transient and socially complex as Soho, where strong decision-making must always be informed by responsiveness to the perpetually shifting nuances of the moment. There is something important about the listening that happens, albeit clumsily, on the king's planet, masked as it is by the outward show of strength. And yet for all its value the king's authority is peculiarly empty. He can react to a new situation by turning an occurrence into an order, demanding a yawn from a Little Prince who is about to fall asleep on his feet. But he lacks the power of initiation. He cannot act decisively or generously. He cannot ease the Little Prince's homesickness by giving him the gift of the extra sunset he craves. He cannot risk anything of himself for others because, living defensively, he has closed himself off to the deep costliness of self-giving. He cannot react with joy or irritation at the Little Prince's endless questions, so great is his

108

preoccupation with maintaining the façade of his own power. There is no room on this planet for dreaming or loving or mistaking or hurting. And so the Little Prince sighs and leaves to continue his quest, recognizing that this king cannot teach him how to manage the vain, demanding flower who has taken root on his planet and in his heart unbidden. And in time I too realized, with some sadness, that this was an inadequate model of authority when dealing with the messiness and the dreams of the real people I was called to love. And so I too moved on.

Arriving eventually on earth, the Little Prince hits crisis point. He comes across a whole field of roses, all of which exactly resemble his own. Having believed his flower when she boasted that she was unique in all the world, he is mortified. The evidence before his eyes suggests that she is, after all, just one flower among millions, no more worthy of his love than any other. Fortunately a fox comes to his rescue. The fox yearns for closeness, so he instructs the Little Prince to tame him. Accordingly, the Little Prince returns every day at exactly the same time, gradually sitting nearer and nearer to his new acquaintance. By the time the taming is complete, they value one another's company so much that when they part for the last time, they cry. Through the fox's guidance, the Little Prince learns the cost of love: the time-consuming effort of forming a deep attachment, and the pain of separation. And he receives a gift of insight. He returns to the field of roses and tells them plainly: 'You are not at all like my rose . . . As yet you are nothing. No one has tamed you, and you have tamed no one.'[2] Through the fox, the Little Prince has learned a critical lesson about his relationship with his flower. It doesn't matter that she resembles all the other roses. What matters is that they have been given to one another, to care and grow together. That fact alone makes her unique, and gives him a unique responsibility. The fox teaches the Little Prince a new kind of authority, based not on rational facts as on the king's planet, but on the powerful vulnerability of being alongside another soul in all their folly and unfolding beauty.

What I find touching about the Little Prince's insight is his recognition that this process has worked both ways. Back home, the

109

flower had tugged at the Prince's heartstrings and challenged him to grow just as much as she had demanded love and care from him. A taming, an adoption, happened between two characters thrown together completely by chance. In the process, both were changed, making them unique to one another and special beyond measure. This is indeed a far cry from the king and his absolute authority. The Prince may technically be in charge of his planet, but through the act of loving he opens himself up to being utterly transformed by the stranger who has quite literally blown in on the wind. The benefits are enormous, but this is, of course, a desperately dangerous way to exercise authority. When a clear-cut hierarchical relationship becomes infused with love, boundaries become fuzzy as a straightforward master/servant relationship gives way to growing interdependence. The joy of love is accompanied by huge emotional and practical costs, demanding of one person the careful relinquishing of a degree of control, and of the other a growing acceptance of new responsibility for themselves and those around them. The quest for flourishing becomes a shared enterprise, demanding of each a new level of self-giving that is both terrifying and exhilarating.

Looking back, I realize that in our small meeting room in Soho, something of this risky, exhilarating love broke through in our midst, blowing apart all my ideas of how authority should best be exercised. For all its bravado, Soho is a holding place for people whose deepest longings have been squashed within mainstream society, and who are seeking ways – healthy or otherwise – to reconnect with themselves and with others. People found their way to the gay scene for all sorts of reasons. Some were just curious, or seeking a cheap thrill. But most people who sought us out had stories to tell about loss and exclusion. Many had been thrown out of families because of their sexuality; others had experienced exclusion in the workplace or in religious communities, or had suffered violence on the streets. Away from all that had limited and confined them, in the safety of our little meeting room, people found space to articulate their pain. As they tapped into the root of their strength and began to support one another, relationships of care formed that bore scant relation to traditional gender roles or barriers of age or culture. So some men found within themselves a maternal gentleness, and some women were freed to enjoy their resilience and forcefulness. It being Soho there was, of course, flamboyance to this – men and women in drag playfully undermined traditional gender roles to outrageous degrees. But behind the carnival atmosphere on these occasions lay vitally important insights. 'Family' formed, as people who would never again belong straightforwardly within traditional patterns of relating found moving ways to reach out and support one another. I was included in this, in gentle and deep recognition of the vulnerability that I too carried. An adoption, a taming took place in the heart of Soho, on the edge of respectability, which opened my heart, released my creativity and enriched me beyond measure.

Where was authority in this? In that small meeting room, words of Jesus on the cross kept ringing in my ears: 'woman, behold your son . . . behold your mother' (John 19.26–27). Humiliated and dying, Jesus calls out to his disciples at the point of their greatest vulnerability, entrusting them to the care of his mother, and entrusting his mother to them. Boundaries disintegrate as Mary becomes mother to children not her own, and they embrace her as their own. But what implications does this have for Jesus' authority? At the point of command, obviously authority rests with him. But after that surely it rests not in a single individual, but rather in the spirit of adoption that he has instigated. From that point on, the authority we claim for ourselves within the Church stands or falls by our willingness to adopt one another, even at the very edge of society and at the limits of personal endurance, so that we and those around us not only survive but grow stronger and more faithful through the most terrible events of our lives. This has long been recognized by commentators who identify these words of Jesus as the point at which the Church comes into being. But its application has historically proved anything but easy. For the team in Soho, the adoptive love that Jesus instigated in his dying moments became a way of life, as we embraced one another in our shared vulnerability and used all the strength at our disposal towards the common good. I have never felt so deeply in tune with the core ministry of the Church as I felt in those years, but nor have I felt so disorientated within its structures. There is a deep and unsettling irony here. The more closely I and my colleagues lived out Jesus' command and made ourselves vulnerable in order to give and receive love on the edges of society, the more we risked censure from within the Church. And as often as not, those who embodied the love I aspired to were the very people who felt they had no place in Christian structures.

There are, of course, good reasons why this kind of authority might be held at arm's length in the Church. Aside from the instinct to hold on to hard-won powers, to exercise authority in this way is to expose oneself to some considerable danger. As a single woman in ministry, I am acutely aware that my very safety, and indeed the safety of those I am called to serve, depends upon my ability to spot the signs that I am being misconstrued, as people mistake openheartedness for sexual availability, or as others, believing I have no significant people in my life, want to establish a relationship of dependency. Engaging with this requires a huge level of prayerful discernment and presence, and it is not unique to those in my position. I have encountered ministers whose marriages have been placed under genuine strain by the inappropriate advances of someone they had been seeking to nurture. And there is another risk too – that of public image. The media is quick to seize upon stories of apparently inappropriate relations of the clergy, and careers are quickly wrecked because a line was perceived to have been crossed. While inappropriate sexual behaviour should obviously never occur in a ministry context, unfortunately for us the words of Jesus demand that other boundaries be crossed all the time. If we take seriously those words from the cross as a decisive moment in the foundation of the Church, then all of us must expose ourselves to the vulnerability of adopting and being adopted. Central to that commission is the gentle, intimate nurture of people who have absolutely no biological, financial or social claim upon us, even – indeed especially – when they are at their most vulnerable. There is simply no way round the risk that this entails, any more than there is a safe or detached way to stand with Mary at the foot of the cross looking up at her crucified son.

Yet the fruits of that risk are tremendous, as the Little Prince teaches us. By the time he finally encounters the author whose plane has broken down in the middle of the desert, he has understood his power. 'If you please – draw me a sheep!' demands the child of the man whose life is in imminent danger as he wrestles with urgent mechanical repairs.[3] And the pilot, dumbfounded, obeys. The Little Prince, blown in from goodness knows where, tames and adopts the man who has also fallen accidentally from the sky. His fearlessness confounds the pilot, who risks a delay to his life-saving repairs while the Prince recalls him to the important things in life, teaching him to care about whether a single sheep a million miles away is properly tethered, and whether a flower lives or dies. Through the Prince's love the man submits to an authority that transcends all rational order and material considerations, and in return he is blessed with salvation in the form of stars that ring with the laughter of a child.

I am convinced that this willingness to stop still, listen and adopt characterizes the very best exercise of authority at the heart of the Church, and enriches it beyond measure. Having myself been blown some considerable distance from worlds away into the heart of the Church, I am profoundly indebted to those brave souls within the institution who have dared to love me in all my complexity, and who continue to impress me with such love and gracious vulnerability that I can no longer withhold anything of my gifting. This is not incidental to the task of good Christian leadership; it is its very substance, and it takes all the spiritual depth and generosity that we have at our disposal. And so I pray that those of us who are privileged to exercise authority in the Church may have the courage to keep hearing and acting on those words from the cross, 'woman, behold . . .' And I pray that we may always be open to the possibility of taming and being tamed, over and over again, by people who yearn for the kind of love that has the power to bring a dead man to life, and that can move a pilot marooned in the desert to care about the fate of a flower a million miles away, veiled in the darkness of the night sky.

I I
'FOR GOD'S SAKE'

Joy Tetley

This is a deliberately ambiguous title. Much depends on how you say it. It is, of course, a very common expletive. As such, it is a vehicle for all kinds of feelings, not least frustration, anger and hurt. In the context of 'women and the Church', and in particular the matter of women as bishops, it can, perhaps, be powerfully expressive of a wide range of views and reactions. Many of us will have heard (or given voice to) comments such as the following:

'For God's sake, get on with it. Just do it.'

'Don't you realize what you're doing, for God's sake? You're destroying the Church.'

'Oh, for God's sake, I've had enough of all this. Let the Church go hang.'

That last comment should give us particular cause for concern. At a time when devotees of atheism are ever more zealously proclaiming their message, the Church of England as by law established is perceived by many as turning in on itself, indeed as turning *on* itself, in self-destructive fervour. Not exactly an attractive option. These are critical times, for the wider community as well as for the Church. So how should we be addressing them, for God's sake?

That question, in fact, points us very much in the direction of the heart of the matter. Many expletives which purloin the name of God or Jesus contain within them, all unrecognized, significant Gospel truth. Our present example is no exception. The Church exists, quite literally, for God's sake – and the sake of God's world. All that we are and do, and the way we do it, should therefore be, first and foremost, for God's sake. That includes, of course, the struggle of our current debate in the Church of England. It matters, for God's sake. Both the process and the outcome really matter. And they do so for profoundly theological reasons (godly reasons). What we in the UK are engaged with at the moment in relation to membership of the episcopate is not, in truth, a distraction. It provides – or should do, if we would but grasp it in this way – a crucial opportunity to explore and express the reality of God.

That should be to the benefit of the world in which we live, not merely a means of sorting out the Church's problems. And, God knows, the world needs such blessing. All God's people, whatever their viewpoint, enjoy the ineffable privilege of being called to participate in God's very life. And that involves responding to the divine imperative to love after the manner of Christ, to work for the proper flourishing of humankind and all creation. A tall order, but an inescapable one if we bear the name of Christ. Whether women should be bishops, and, so to speak, on what terms, belongs very much in this context.

What is at issue here, if mere mortals may frame it thus, is no less than who God is, how God operates, and what God's purposes might be. This is our overarching and urgent agenda. We need to make that emphatically clear. In such a cause, I attempt to pursue this comprehensive theological agenda just a little, and primarily from my perspective as a biblical explorer. In particular, I want to highlight some themes, which I believe are highly pertinent, from a New Testament writing that has received strangely little attention in this whole controversy about women and the Church.

First, some core observations. However well crafted and thought out our doctrinal words and formulae might be, they cannot pin down the enormity of the mystery who is God. As St Augustine succinctly put it, 'If you have comprehended, *what* you have comprehended is not God.' There has always been a strong apophatic dimension in the life, experience and teaching of the Church, stressing that God is far greater than all our attempts at definition and explanation. Even the credal statements are bursting with possibilities beyond our rational ken. We might acknowledge, far more often than we do perhaps, that God should reduce us to silence.

Yet God has spoken. And God has invited us into passionate relationship – relationship characterized by the exchange of love and the *exploration* of love. In living, loving relationships, there is always more to be discovered – if only we are open to listen, and adventurous enough to risk our security. Faith seeks understanding – not certainty.

The scriptures bear powerful witness to this truth. They disclose a tantalizing God; a God who will not be tamed or confined; a God who breaks out of boundaries, even sacred boundaries; a God who constantly surprises and challenges, yet is utterly trustworthy and faithful; a God whose burning holiness takes God into the middle of the messiness of the world; a God whose passionate love puts God on the receiving end of savage abuse; a God bursting with creativity, vitality and joy, who nonetheless weeps with those who weep; a God who is greater than all that is, yet with a personal touch that is awesome in its intensity.[1] God, in essence, is pure and absolute *love*. All else flows from this. Love is God's motivation, God's modus operandi, God's mission. What might this mean?

It certainly means the primacy of relationship. Throughout the scriptural narratives, there is a dialogue going on – a dialogue between God and humankind and humankind and God. It is a dialogue characterized by passion, on both sides. Strong feelings abound, whether of joy and delight or of hurt and anger. The conversation is rarely a superficial one, though it can be very mundane in form. Sometimes it is far from polite (witness Job, for example). Yet in such tempestuous exchange is rich relationship born. Divine love is a full-blooded affair. And in its expression, blood is willingly and painfully shed. In the scriptures we encounter, 'in many and various ways', the God who is, at heart, the God of cross and resurrection; the God who comes to us where we are and goes to hell and back with us and for us; the God who will go to any lengths to open up the fulfilment of love's potential – including stretching the 'rules' to breaking point.

We see this very clearly in the letter to the Hebrews. This radical New Testament document has not featured largely in the debate about women and the Church. It has been, at best, marginal to the discussion. Indeed, it has tended to be somewhat marginal to New Testament studies as a whole, let alone to the attention of theologians more generally. That is perhaps fitting for a 'word of exhortation' (as it calls itself, Heb. 13.22) that sees God setting aside mainstream (God-given) tradition and following through a marginal thread – not because of divine obstreperousness but in passionate pursuit of God's mission of love. It is this latter which is of key importance. It therefore demands attention from those who, in any sense, would be God's ministers.

Hebrews is no abstract theological treatise. Like most of the rest of the New Testament, it is, as it were, 'circumstantial theology' – provoked into articulation by the pressure of actualities, practicalities, *circum-stances*; theology grappled with, of necessity, on the way ('synodically,' one might almost literally say). It was as our earliest Christian forebears followed 'on the way' that they were impelled by *what happened* to engage on every level of being with the tantalizing calling of a tantalizing God. Along the twists and turns of the way, through confusion and questioning, misunderstanding and lostness, tears and heartbreak, they came to a new way of seeing, a vision beyond their imagining at the outset, and an urgent mission to a world both sceptical and credulous. This is not an easy way to do theology. But it does lead somewhere – and somewhere very significant.

In the case of Hebrews, the community addressed (whoever and wherever they were) were clearly in a very hard place on their faith journey – to the deep concern of the person writing to them. Whoever that was desperately wanted to give them an injection of courage and fresh vision. They were disheartened to the point of giving up, overwhelmed by the effects of hostility and opposition. It seems that this expression of the body of Christ was in serious danger of falling apart, threatened, not least, by what Hebrews describes as the 'root of bitterness' (Heb. 12.15) taking hold in the soil of fear. Their experience is not perhaps unique, as today's Anglican Communion might very well bear witness.

The one trying to get through to them in this parlous situation urges them to endurance. The exhortation to 'hang on in there' permeates what is, in effect, a sermon for a time of crisis. But the preacher realizes that just telling them to persevere is not enough. They need to be reminded of why they should bother to try. They need to be re-energized and re-focused in their relationship with God. They need to 'see Jesus' afresh.

So the preacher opens for them *a new vision of Jesus* which is no less than stunning. It is both profoundly encouraging and deeply challenging. Like God. Indeed, Hebrews intends there to be no doubt that when God's people look to Jesus, they see into the heart of God. The magnificent opening sentence (covering the first four verses of our English translation) says it all:

Long ago God spoke to our ancestors in many and various ways by the prophets, but in these last days he has spoken to us in a Son, whom he appointed heir of all things, through whom also he created the worlds. He is the reflection of God's glory and the exact imprint of God's very being and he sustains all things by his powerful word. When he had made purification for sins, he sat down at the right hand of the Majesty on high, having become as much superior to angels as the name he has inherited is more excellent than theirs. (Heb. 1.1–4)

As Richard Bauckham succinctly puts it, here is an 'overwhelming emphasis on the full and eternal deity of the Son'.[2] The one who is Son shares the divine identity, creativity, glory and grace.

This Son, whom we encounter as Jesus, is, in truth, the 'character' of God (1.3), 'the same, yesterday, today and for ever' (13.8). If God's people want to know who God is and how God operates, then it is indeed to Jesus that they must look. What they see will both put fresh courage into them and challenge some deeply held assumptions.

That is particularly so when they contemplate Jesus as the 'great High Priest', who fleshes out 'once and for all' a priestly ministry that is both divine and definitive. As Bauckham underlines, 'this high priesthood, unlike the Levitical, does belong to the unique identity of God'.[3] Here is the absolutely effective self-expression of God's priestly yearning for intimate communion with all. Only Hebrews among the New Testament writers presents us with such an explicit and extended portrayal of the 'godly priesthood' of Jesus.

This is radical territory. Whoever those addressed by Hebrews were, it seems clear that they had close associations with Jewish tradition. They would be familiar, therefore, with the levitical priestly provision believed to have been made by God to enable an appropriate measure of safe communion. In that context, seeing Jesus as great high priest presented a major theological – and, indeed, ecclesiological – obstacle. The preacher not only recognizes this but regards it as integral to his perception of the way God works. The matter is concisely expressed at the heart of the sermon's argument:

Now if perfection had been attainable through the levitical priesthood – for the people received the law under this priesthood – what further need would there have been to speak of another priest arising according to the order of Melchizedek, rather than one according to the order of Aaron? For when there is a change in the priesthood, there is necessarily a change in the law as well. Now the one of whom these things are spoken belonged to another tribe, from which no one has ever served at the altar. For it is evident that our Lord was descended from Judah, and in connection with that tribe, Moses said nothing about priests. (Heb. 7.11–14)

The incarnate self-expression of God was breaking the rules of the sacred assembly, the rules of a sacred order instituted by God. Jesus was not qualified to be a priest. His priesthood flies in the face of the received tradition of generations. Here is God exercising the divine prerogative to do a new thing – to be original, innovative, creative – bursting boundaries in order for divine love to have its full impact – reshaping and redefining a tradition that can only have meaning insofar as it ministers God's saving grace. As Ellingworth points out, 'God has the sovereign right to change "the priesthood"'.[4] In Christ, that is precisely what God has done. It is not, of course, that God has, so to speak, got it wrong in its earlier version. It is, rather, that because of human frailty and fallenness, it remained but a shadow of what it could be. So God has opened up a new avenue (a 'new and living way', 10.20) to enable the fundamental purpose behind the tradition to be fully realized.

That purpose, for Hebrews, is best understood through the fulfilment of a bedrock divine promise – that of a new covenant (cf. Jer. 31.31ff.). Hebrews quotes it at length (the only New Testament writer to do so):

> This is the covenant that I will make with the house of Israel after those days, says the Lord. I will put my laws in their minds, and write them on their hearts, and I will be their God, and they shall be my people. And they shall not teach one another or say to each other, 'Know the Lord', for they shall all know me, from the least of them to the greatest. For I will be merciful towards their iniquities, and I will remember their sins no more. (Heb. 8.10–12)

In speaking of 'a new covenant', says Hebrews, God 'has made the first one obsolete' (Heb. 8.13).

Hallowed tradition, it seems, *can* be set aside, in the interests of releasing more completely the truth that prompted its formulation in the first place. 'They shall all know me', says the Lord, 'from the least of them to the greatest . . . I will remember their sins no more.' Here is the 'knowing', not so much of information *about* God as of intimate relationship *with* God – a relationship that God intends should be open to all, without distinction. At the very throne of grace, everyone belongs and everyone is of equal standing. Such is the imperative of God's mission. Direct access into God's very presence comes through God's direct action in Jesus. The prophecy of a new covenant and the essential 'raison d'être' of priesthood are integrated and fulfilled.

It is the sacrificial, priestly love of God in Jesus that makes this possible. Through an unorthodox priest, consigned and killed 'outside the camp' (Heb. 13.11–13), outside the boundaries of the holy, come world-transforming consequences. What is at first seen as shameful (Heb. 12.2) carries the costly creativity of God, bearing fruit in the offer of full and free communion, characterized by forgiveness, mercy and grace. All that is needed in response is to 'draw near'. And though others might point the way, no intermediaries are necessary. If they will, all can approach God with confidence, for themselves (Heb. 4.16; 10.19–22).

Through an unorthodox priest . . . yes – but it is also the insight of Hebrews that the irregular priesthood of Jesus was not without its traditional pointers. God might be doing a new thing, but off centre stage there had been tangential signals. Jesus is a high priest 'after the order of Melchizedek'. This king/priest Melchizedek is a mysterious and marginal figure, mentioned only twice in the canonical Hebrew scriptures (Gen. 14.18–20 and Ps. 110.4). He was, indeed, an outsider, not even a member of God's chosen people. Yet it is this figure from the edges of tradition who, for Hebrews, provides the paradigm for God's decisive intervention in Jesus. Melchizedek contributed dimensions that the mainstream Aaronic priests could not (see especially Heb. 7).

Melchizedek's priesthood was of a different and superior order, rendering him greater even than Abraham, the founding patriarch of God's people. Not only did his name and title express the messianic qualities of righteousness and peace, but also, Hebrews asserts, using a common form of argument from silence, 'he is without father or mother or genealogy'. In terms of the levitical tradition, based firmly and without exception on genealogical credentials, Melchizedek did not qualify for membership of the priestly order. But for Hebrews such a genealogical deficit means in fact that Melchizedek 'has neither beginning of days nor end of life, but resembling the Son of God he continues a priest for ever' (7.3). The Melchizedekian priesthood thus points in the direction of that divine priestly character that finds focal expression in Jesus and cannot be confined or defined, even by centuries of undoubtedly holy tradition. In this sense, and by enabling vital insight into God's sovereign freedom and boundless love, Melchizedek's time had come.

It is tempting to end by saying, 'Let the reader understand.' Certainly I would argue that Hebrews' particular theological insights need to be fed into any discussions about the nature of God and God's working, very much including that relating to women and leadership. Hebrews, after all, is undeniably part of the sacred tradition, integral to the canonical scriptures. Its perspectives matter, therefore, and have crucial things to speak into the Church's debating and discerning. Our present arguing should most definitely be in the context of who God is, how God operates – and why. As suggested above, Hebrews can take something of a searchlight to that. If God behaved as Hebrews perceived in the supremely indicative act of the incarnation, that must surely tell us something rather important about the essential modus operandi of God. Jesus Christ (the self-expression of God) is 'the same yesterday, today and for ever'. That means he is ever the 'pioneer' (Heb. 2.10; 12.2), the risk-taker, the boundary crosser. It means also that tradition, however holy, is not God. It can be changed, and for very good, indeed holy, reasons. 'Where there is a change in the priesthood, there is necessarily a change in the law as well', Hebrews reminds us (7.13), that is, in the way the things of God are understood and practised. But that 'change' by no means dispenses with the fundamental meaning and intention of the ministry that has gone before. God's essential purposes have not changed. They are brought to fruition and new possibilities are opened up. Such change is, however, messy, painful and disturbing, demanding a radical shift in perspective and the courage to continue on a risky and exploratory path, leading outside the hitherto defined boundaries of the camp. This is new territory, and the only map is in the shape of a cross. But look what emerged from that confusion, darkness and mess – the explosion of Easter and Pentecost. Look to Jesus – and why he endured all that shame and pain. No less than for God's sake, and the sake of God's world. God's people, called to be 'partners of Christ' (3.14), must be prepared to embrace that demanding vocational imperative. They may then discover, with Jesus, the joy that is set before them (12.2).

12

EVANGELICAL WOMEN, SPIRITUALITY AND LEADERSHIP

Elizabeth A. Hoare

This Christmas I listened to yet another sermon preached by a man about the Virgin Mary conceiving and bearing a son (Luke 1). He was doing his best to be faithful to the text but his description of Mary's reaction bore no resemblance whatsoever to my own experience of childbearing. Preaching is held in very high regard by almost all evangelicals, and until recently has been a largely male preserve. The increasing number of evangelical women occupying pulpits is just one of the ways that evangelical spirituality is being changed by women in positions of leadership in the Church today. This is not universally the case, however, hence the title of this chapter.

That sermon was, I believe, symptomatic of what happens when concern for the authority of the Bible leads to downplaying the place of human experience, especially women's experience. First, however, it is important to set out the key characteristics of evangelical spirituality and there are three foundational ones that will be the driving force of what is said here. Evangelical spirituality is Bible-based, it is cross-centred, focusing on the life, death and resurrection of Jesus Christ, and it is activist and outward-looking in mission.

Alongside the books and journals I have read and the public addresses I have listened to, many of my observations about evangelicals and leadership have arisen out of the ministry of spiritual direction. It is here that men and women feel safe enough to articulate what they really think and feel. Many of the issues that arise for men and women struggling to be faithful to Christ arise because of a Church that does not enable either to be themselves.

Today spiritual direction is as much the preserve of the laity both in the giving and receiving of it. Among evangelicals the word 'mentoring' is often preferred and may mean something rather different, but one-to-one discipling of some kind has always been part of the evangelical tradition. Why so many are seeking spiritual direction today may seem far removed from the subject of this book, but I believe it is connected to the problems facing a Church that does not appear 'spiritual'. Spiritual direction is increasingly sought by people disaffected with the Church but who have not lost their faith, and this includes evangelicals. It is also sought by people who are seeking God but who may not have any religious language to articulate what it is they are looking for and who would not wish to go to church to learn it. Some are put off by what they perceive as an institution hostile to women. Others object to the feminized image of the Church. Both perceptions cry out for increased efforts to move to the kind of equality that the God of the Bible desires.

Spiritual direction does not seem to be a leadership issue. It can be, and often is, exercised by lay people. It is personal and private and hidden from the public domain. It can be perceived, however, as being somewhat esoteric and even elitist. One essential result of embracing women as well as men in leadership in the Church would be to put a stop to the temptation to withdraw from bodily and worldly reality into mystical experiences so that spirituality may become the embodied experience that it is for the whole Church.

Spiritual direction is relational by its very nature. It involves two people listening together to a third, the Holy Spirit, who is the real director. In her important book on spiritual direction,

Holy Listening, Margaret Guenther offers three models of this ministry. They are spiritual direction as midwifery, spiritual direction as hospitality and spiritual direction as teaching.[1] While each of these models may appear at first sight to be more female than male in orientation, the biblical sources of the images remind us that midwives may be very assertive (for example, Ex. 1.15–21), hospitality is not just about women in the kitchen (Gen. 18.1–15) and teaching in the New Testament was provided by women and men (Acts 18.24–26).

Evangelicals begin with scripture. We often think we are the only ones who take scripture seriously, which of course is not true, but evangelicals have a particular way of approaching scripture that we are not prepared to see undermined. The authority of the Bible must always take precedence, and for Anglican evangelicals that means that scripture has authority over reason and tradition, though of course the latter are vital for its interpretation. Most important of all, the Bible takes precedence over experience. This means that some evangelicals are suspicious of aspects of spirituality because it is understood to be about experience. Spiritual direction and theological reflection, for example, necessarily take human experience seriously as the arena where God is, and there are evangelical contributions in these areas that need to be heard and enabled to join in the conversation. It is important to acknowledge the discomfort evangelicals have when experience is set on a par with the Bible, because many if not most of the arguments in support of women exercising leadership are rendered invalid as far as some more conservative evangelicals are concerned. Evangelicals at this end of the spectrum will never be won over to the vital importance of women in leadership with arguments based on sociology, culture or even justice. The justification of women exercising leadership must be grounded in the Bible. That there are excellent biblical grounds for welcoming women into full leadership along with men needs to be understood by evangelicals and non-evangelicals alike for the benefit of the whole Church. God's word does not need protecting from social and cultural insight, but the conversation needs to take place.

Spirituality concerns the way we live out what we believe about God. Evangelicals emphasize discipleship, though they are not always as good at helping people to keep going in their walk with God as they are at introducing them to him in the first place.[2] Discipleship involves far more than knowing the right answers to life's questions, and whatever beliefs and head knowledge we carry around must be able to inform and activate daily living. Spirituality is based fundamentally on fostering a relationship with God and evangelicalism owes a great deal to its pietist ancestors who drew attention to the relational aspect of Christianity and its emotional expression. 'New men' apart, words like relational and spirituality are often interpreted as predominantly female. I am wary, however, of stereotypes of what is male and what is female, so I am reluctant to say that women are better at feelings or even that they are more comfortable with images of leadership as nurturing. Nevertheless, experience of women in leadership roles in the wider Church so far does suggest that they prefer a collaborative approach to leadership and are less concerned with issues of status and hierarchy. Indeed, as in other parts of the Church where there are evangelical women in leadership (often in other traditions), they tend not to be visible or recognized.

There is not a great deal in evangelical spirituality that makes women in positions of leadership spring to mind. Until recently its heroes have been mostly men and its activist nature was not open to women for whom the home was the arena where spirituality was lived out. We have to turn to the foreign mission field to find women who were very active indeed but not visible and, safely abroad, could be ignored. Biblical scholarship has uncovered role models in scripture for all women to embrace, and evangelicals, along with others, are indebted to feminist insights that have recovered the hidden voices of women in the Bible. Similarly, recent approaches to historical research have restored the place of women in evangelical history and reminded us of their great contribution in mission and evangelism.

Spirituality and scripture are intimately connected and nourish each other. The renewal, in the second half of the twentieth

127

century, of the conviction that biblical studies should be spiritually relevant means that the voices of evangelical men and women who believe that women should be exercising leadership within the Church are a rich source for understanding what the Spirit is saying to the churches today through the words of the Bible.

Evangelical women have particular hurdles to get over before we are to see them alongside men in Christian leadership. The obvious one is that a powerful component of the evangelical constituency does not believe that they should be there and points to scripture as incontestable evidence of this fact. It does not appear likely that many conservative evangelicals will ever budge on this issue, though some would concede that it is among those things deemed *adiaphora*, even if they could not accept women as incumbents. Disregarding the complicated textual issues of 1 Timothy 2.12 (that women should not teach or have authority over men) and its multiple possible meanings, and despite other clear references to women in leadership in the writings of St Paul, and a great deal of exegetical work having been done to uncover New Testament women exercising authoritative roles, the headship issue remains the sticking point. It is not an incontestable argument, however, and it is important to recognize a variety of attitudes towards women in leadership among evangelicalism as a whole.

Is it possible to envisage a time when some of the larger evangelical churches have women leaders? It will require biblical thinking that is open to change akin to the huge change that Acts 10 describes when the Gentiles were recognized as equal partners in the gospel. Alongside evangelical women in leadership, my own conviction is that we also need more evangelical women theologians and biblical scholars who will encourage thinking and writing from their perspective.

There are other questions surrounding the way evangelicals approach the Bible that have a bearing on the place of women. Many sermons and leadership courses turn to biblical examples for instruction and inspiration: Moses, David, Elijah, Peter, Paul and so on. These are flawed heroes, and evangelicals learn from their mistakes as well as their successes, but they are all male. When we look for females they are there, but naturally they are not held up as icons of leadership. The most serious omission is Mary. Evangelicals have been so spooked by the Roman Catholic veneration of Mary that she is often ignored altogether. We need to recover Mary and learn from her in fresh ways. For example, the story of the Visitation presents us with two women who delight in each other's worth and recognize the promise of God that has been bestowed on them both. Mary, full of the Holy Spirit says: 'The Almighty has done great things for me.' Her identity and self-worth is rooted in God, not in any achievement of her own. She does not steal the limelight either from God or from her companion. Women are relational and they bring this to what they do. If the churches modelled leadership like this the results would be manifest for all to see. Here is a quality of leadership the Church desperately needs.

If evangelicals are prone to play down the place of Mary in God's scheme of things, poor Joseph has dropped off the radar altogether.[3] Yet he too would repay some deeper biblical reflection. Evangelicals will tend to say that in a marriage it is the man who is the head, but who had authority in Jesus' home when he was a child? Before we rush to defend male headship or make pious statements about Jesus, we have to recall that the latter 'was obedient' to his parents (Luke 2.51) and Joseph humbly accepted that Mary's calling was superior to his claims on her. He responded by remaining in the background, usually the woman's role in traditional evangelical homes. Like his future wife, Joseph submitted humbly to God even though it meant surrendering his traditional superiority. The Church is so quick to think in terms of hierarchy, but in this home each person had a unique role and was essential to the unfolding of God's plan. Indeed the roles of Jesus, Mary and Joseph point us to the non-hierarchical view of relationships expressed in Ephesians 5.21–33 which refers to the ordering of the household. This passage is usually used to stress the primacy of the husband in the marriage relationship, but by doing so neglects verse 2, which prefaces all that follows. ('Be subject to one another out of reverence for Christ.') This way of looking at the passage would be in accord with Galatians 3.28, which clearly states that we have been made equal through the redeeming love of Christ. Alongside the serious wrestling with those passages that appear to assign women a subordinate role, especially in the Church, the rest of scripture also needs to be engaged with critically to allow other voices to be heard as well.

Another issue facing evangelical men and women who believe in women exercising authority in the Church is the old school tie. Networks are strong and it is difficult for women to break in to them at every level. There are deep issues around power at work here and evangelicals need to do some hard thinking about what the Bible says about power. Even among those who say that they do believe in women having authority there is a reluctance to take the plunge and appoint them. Is this because they fear peer disapproval or simply that there are not enough jobs and the available ones go to the men first because they are known? From then on the structures of the Church work against women breaking in. Women tend not to go to conferences where networking takes place and they are therefore less visible. As a consequence of all this there are fewer role models around for women to observe and be inspired by. This point is crucial for changing the culture around women in leadership and has faced the Church from the moment it was agreed to ordain women to the priesthood. If evangelical women feel that they have to be honorary men, the argument for complementarity is defeated.[4] This situation breeds and perpetuates a certain kind of spirituality too. This male-centred world has particular ways of dealing with power and vulnerability.

Conservative evangelicalism tends to be more deeply indebted to the Enlightenment than it is prepared to admit: logical and intellectual in its expression and wary of anything regarded as 'touchy-feely'. This reinforces a 'them and us attitude' to what should be open to all. Women can operate at a cerebral level and do not always approach God from their experience, but the stereotype often wins out and the spirituality of whole congregations is skewed as a result. A number of churches across the evangelical constituency do have women on the staff but they are not ordained, or if they are they hold junior positions. So these churches might claim to believe in equality of leadership but they are clearly sending out a different message. Perhaps there is a fear that having a woman in charge will undermine the traditional role she has had in the home. Our rapidly changing world means rather that we need to return again and again to assumptions and look at them in the light of scripture in conversation with experience. The experience of women facing the challenges head-on would be an invaluable resource in helping the whole Church to sound the depths of what is good in those traditional roles and what is not.

And what of the cross, the other central feature of evangelicalism so far only mentioned implicitly? Sermon after sermon has reminded me that the ground at the foot of the cross is level and we are all equal. Sadly, as an ordained woman I have not found it to be so in the Church. When it comes to leading the people in remembrance of that revolutionary event that subverts all our categories, the ground is very unequal indeed. The early evangelicals set great store by Holy Communion and urged its frequent celebration. In many evangelical churches today it is neglected, and when it is celebrated it is often tacked on to the end of the main service. This means that the emphasis on the corporate experience of Christ who has overcome all evil, sin and injustice and who beckons us forward to anticipate the heavenly banquet where all hierarchy is meaningless is either lacking or is located in the pulpit where words and logical argument take the place of symbol. For evangelicals everything is to be filtered through the redeeming work of Christ on the cross. This must include our humanity and all our human relating. Though we await the completion of the new order, the old has been overthrown and we are called to anticipate as far as possible God's future. This means that the spiritual freedom we have been given in Christ must call into question both sins of pride and sins of self-effacement. Far from causing chaos – emasculating men and turning women into dominatrices – God's intention for men and women is to enable us to be ourselves, equal and complementary. Christian spirituality would flourish in a way that would draw outsiders to want to know more and so facilitate the evangelical imperative to spread the good news.

Evangelism has changed as a result of the focus on experience. We are told again and again that it is vital to start where people are. Bombarding people with prepositional truth will not win many souls. Sharing our stories, journeying with people who are seeking, looking for bridges to build and points of contact is much more likely to gain a hearing. The international Alpha course is set within the context of hospitality and makes space for discussion. It works best when people's comments and questions are taken seriously and genuine interaction takes place. In the UK the CPAS (Church Pastoral Aid Society) course 'Essence' is different again and relies on sensory experience and imagination as much as imparting facts.

Evangelicals may rejoice at this because it is much closer to the evangelistic style of both the apostle Paul and Jesus himself.[5] An increasing number of books on spirituality are concerned with finding God in the ordinary. These often focus on the domestic and we still need more books around work issues and the prevailing values of western society, but at least spirituality is recognized as having to do with the whole of life and not just a small spiritual compartment. Spiritual direction might centre on prayer but prayer never takes place in a vacuum and thus the stuff of experience is relevant to what is talked about.

Women have always shared experience of course, usually while undertaking domestic tasks and childcare, but certainly in evangelical circles it has too often remained a mystery to men and the subject of tired mother-in-law jokes from the pulpit or patronizing allusions to home life. A spirituality of mutual respect based on the recognition of God in all things might be one significant result of seeing evangelical women in positions of leadership.

Talking about the stuff of spiritual experience is concerned both with nurturing and evangelism. The Christian faith is relational, and that means something to people today.

I omitted a fourth feature of evangelical spirituality noted by David Bebbington, namely conversion. It is often regarded as a once-and-for-all experience by evangelicals, but most of us recognize the need for turning again and again away from our sinful selves and towards the newness of life in God. It requires an openness to being changed and is therefore full of hope for those who long to see change not only in themselves but in the Church too.

Leadership is still too closely bound up with ideas of power and control. Only when women are given positions of leadership on an equal footing with men will they be in a place where they can construct another paradigm. This is as true for evangelical women as it is for the rest of the Church, but evangelicals in particular need to see more women modelling what leadership could look like from a more equal perspective.

This requires both men and women taking risks. It will mean men being willing to give up power and control. It will mean women rejecting any retreat into self-effacement while refusing to give in to the temptation to use power in old familiar ways. It would also mean other parts of the Church taking risks with evangelicals who are sometimes excluded from discussions, having been prejudged not to want to participate. Some of us do want to do so and believe that we have something constructive to offer, as well as many things to learn.

PART 4

THE CHARACTER OF THE FUTURE

13

WHAT CLERGY DO, ESPECIALLY WHEN IT LOOKS LIKE NOTHING

Emma Percy

There is a wonderful book about the early years of mothering by Naomi Stadlen, called *What Mothers Do, Especially When it Looks Like Nothing*.[1] Stadlen is interested in the lack of language we have to talk meaningfully about what a mother of a young child is doing with all her time. How is it, she wonders, that an exhausted new mother can claim to have been doing nothing all day?

> Nothing? Has the time simply 'gone'? Even now, as we look at her, you and I can clearly see that she is being present for her baby. She has given up her shower and her lunch. She is devoting her time and energy to him. We are looking at a baby who is being generously mothered. But most people would find it hard to explain this. Our language can be very clear and precise about anything practical. A person who has 'tidied up' has both the words and a tidy area to show for it. It is much harder to find a word that describes the giving-up-things mode of attention a mother is giving to her baby. Often there is no obvious visible change in the baby to confirm that she has made any difference.[2]

Stadlen sees this lack of language as a particular problem for women today who become mothers after being in professional jobs. They are used to being able to articulate clearly what they do, they may well be able to point to projects completed and goals achieved; how different when they move into the world of nurturing care where tasks are more cyclical and it is much harder to measure what is achieved. She argues that mothering is under-articulated and therefore undervalued. She claims that we have a vocabulary for when mothering is done badly but not for when it is done well, and this means that mothers can find it hard to explain to themselves what they have been doing all day, let alone to other people.

How can anyone feel satisfied at the end of a day doing something as responsible as being a mother, without being able to explain to herself what she has done well? How can she discuss her day properly with other people if she can only describe her failures? This has a practical implication. If women perceive mothering as unsatisfying, will they enjoy doing it?[3]

I find some very interesting parallels between these comments of Stadlen's about mothering and the role of parish clergy. One of the problems for those engaged in parish ministry, especially when that is the full-time job, is in the lack of language to explain adequately what it is that clergy do. Anthony Russell's *The Clerical Profession* and, more recently, Martyn Percy in *Clergy: The Origin of Species* explore how the historical development of professions, and the self-understanding of clergy as a profession, has strangely brought an uncertainty about how to define the clerical role.[4] Percy quotes Urban Holmes' account of a conversation with a Lutheran pastor.

The question is asked, 'What is your profession?' The reply is, 'Well, I'm something like a "counsellor", but not really. I'm more a "teacher" but not in a formal sense. Maybe you could say I'm interested in change, but not quite like anyone else.' The point is that in pursuit of professional status we have divested ourselves of a different kind of symbolic role, without ever resolving the question as to what precisely our unique professional competence might be. Every time we think we have come up with an answer, someone has been there before us.[5]

Clearly this Lutheran pastor is trying to find a way of explaining what he does in terms of other kinds of professions, yet it seems he cannot find a satisfactory language not simply because 'someone' has got there first, but also because nothing seems to describe the role adequately. Another problem is that if he or a Church of England vicar tries to sit down and describe what it is they do, it may well sound ineffectual and not like a proper job. Percy also quotes from a 1970s report on clergy by Towler and Coxon.

Now the clergyman, more than anyone else on the contemporary scene, is a jack of all trades. He occupies a unique position, but the uniqueness of his position has nothing to do with unique skills, or even with unique competence . . . He does not have a job at all in any sense which is readily understandable today, and today, more than ever before, a person must have a job in order to fit into society.[6]

Here the parallels with mothering are interesting, as both struggle to articulate the role they fulfil, which is not a job like other jobs. It is also, for both, complicated by the fact that people take on aspects of these roles full-time and part-time. Others who may themselves spend the majority of their time in more easily definable jobs competently do some of what parish clergy do. In terms of mothering, Stadlen is interested at how to begin to find different ways of talking about the things that mothers do. She is particularly interested in how little language we have to describe the skills mothers learn through their practice. This lack of the right language is, I maintain, part of the problem for clergy. There is not an easy language to talk about many aspects of being a vicar. It is possible to talk about many different tasks involved. It is possible to talk theologically about

139

ministering sacraments and living incarnationally. Yet many of the skills good parish clergy learn, practise and develop are under-articulated and consequently may lead to clergy feeling under-valued. It therefore seems important, for those who have the responsibility of care for parish clergy, to find constructive ways of articulating and celebrating the skills of good ordinary parish ministry. Perhaps a few examples will begin to explore the kinds of things I am alluding to.

Like many clergy, I recently took a funeral for a man I did not know. I sat with his family round the kitchen table and we talked about him; I listened and made notes. I wasn't simply listening to the words but to the atmosphere – the way people spoke about him. A few days later we met in the crematorium and I gave back to them, in words, a picture of the man they had known and loved. People congratulated the son on the words they assumed he had written for me and he explained that he hadn't. As on numerous occasions, I used the skills I have learned and developed through the practice of ministry. There is no specific terminology to explain this skill, which involves attentive listening, careful distilling, the creation in my head of a relationship with a man I never knew, so that when I talk to them about him he feels real to me. Yet despite its namelessness I know that this skill, which I share with so many clergy, is deeply valued by those we minister to. Over time it can feel effortless and yet it demands concentration and energy and can at times leave me feeling drained. Those beyond the Church recognize it and admire it as a skill, but those who appraise clergy or who write about what clergy do rarely comment on it.

Another clerical skill is the incredible ability parish clergy have to move constantly between very different circumstances and modes of being. So one moment a priest is comforting a grieving widow, then the next appointment involves singing silly songs with the toddler group; then on to visiting various people who may be unwell, housebound or simply lonely; and then chairing a meeting about the church hall finances. Even in this sentence I use the term 'comforting' as if it is self-evident what that entails. It is in fact a complex and nuanced skill that when well used can help people through some of the most difficult experiences. It is an immensely important skill for those engaged in priestly ministry, but I don't recall ever being asked if I was good at comforting people. The variety of encounters in a given day can be stimulating, but it takes a particular kind of skill to be moving constantly between these situations and to be genuinely and appropriately present in each. Each involves what Stadlen calls 'the giving-up-things mode of attention' (see quote above). Each person encountered requires attentive listening and thoughtful conversation; we never quite know when something may be said that is deeply personal and needs careful sensitive handling. As the vicar you are representing not simply yourself but the Church, the Christian faith and in some aspect God himself. The mixture of emotions stirred up by each encounter needs to be held and not spilt inappropriately in the next. The difficult things heard must be carried and perhaps shared only in prayer with God. From the outside it can look like lots of cups of tea and cosy chats, but the reality is so much more when the priest is able to exercise well the pastoral skills she has learned through the careful practice of caring ministry. It is not easy to quantify what has been achieved by all the mixed encounters of a typical clergy day in the parish. Sometimes the value of a visit can feel tangible, at other times we may never know how important our being in each of those places has been. What is clear is that it has taken time and energy and there is a skill to this moving from one thing to another and holding the myriad cares.

Other aspects of the vicar's role may seem well articulated, yet they may not do justice to all that is going on. There is plenty of material about the skills involved in leading worship, preaching and teaching. Yet even here there seems to be so much that matters that is difficult to put into words. For instance, how do we describe the way a good vicar is able to scrutinize the congregation carefully, noting who is absent, who is new or rarely seen, who looks distressed or distracted, while at the same time leading the service with dignity and care? How do we describe the skills necessary to say the right things at the end of a service

141

as people leave, the comments that make people feel known and valued? Over time these skills become almost unthinking, yet we know that they are part of why, when we at last sit down on our own, we feel drained of energy. We also know that when they are well used, the congregation feels well cared for. Parish clergy need to carry so much in their heads, from the practical aspects of maintaining church buildings and the ongoing worshipping life of the church, to the myriad facts about parishioners' lives. Clergy really do at times feel like a jack of all trades. Things are rarely finished and even the satisfying tasks that are simply make space for more that must be done.

How do we adequately articulate and explain the way in which clergy help to build up and sustain the community of the congregation, finding ways to value the difficult, to care for the unlovely as well as all those who are a joy and delight? No priest is perfect and each of us works within the particularity of a given community, but so many clergy work hard to sustain and nurture congregations made up of a variety of people who might not normally be easily knit together. There are many more aspects of ordinary parish ministry that could be explored to highlight the under-articulated skills of the job. In this short chapter I am not trying to describe all that clergy do, but I wish to stress the importance of finding ways to celebrate these many skills and affirm those who have developed them and continue to practise and hone them. This is not easy because our patterns of ministry still tend towards one priest working in his or her parish or parishes. Other practitioners do not often see you in action, and the insecurity of clergy can mean that sharing one's successes and failures with other clergy needs relationships of trust that are not always easy to find. Congregations and the wider community may well appreciate what they have, but, as with mothering, when it is going well it can seem effortless and natural. So much of what clergy do is invisible and intangible and plenty of it can be taken for granted.

There has been in writing about the role of parish clergy over the years what I think is a false dichotomy between being and doing. Many of the things that clergy do that I think need better articulation are associated with the way they are with people and in situations, and thus could fall into ideas about ministry that stress an incarnational model of 'being' there. Yet what I want to say is that 'being' in ministry involves a lot of 'doing'. It involves carrying out necessary tasks, many of which are ongoing and mundane, some of which are sacred – and yet even the sacred tasks involve ongoing practical, repetitive things that must be done. There are times when all these day-to-day or week-to-week tasks are rewarding and satisfying and times when they are irksome or simply mundane. They are complexly intermingled with the creation and maintenance of webs of relationships, which involve the use of many carefully acquired skills, some of which I have highlighted above. The grace given in ordination makes us priests, but that does not take away the fact that we have to learn how to be priests through all that we do in relationship to the people entrusted to us. Our own characters and previous experiences will mean that some things come easier than others, but because so many aspects of what we do are difficult to define it can be hard to acknowledge what has been well learned, and difficult to name what needs improving.

It seems to me that those engaged in episcope, ministry that involves the oversight and care of parish clergy, need to think seriously about how we can better articulate and value the day-to-day skills of parish ministry. In doing so it may become easier to affirm good parish ministry and helpfully critique areas that need improvement. Clearly this is one of the intentions of ministerial reviews or appraisal systems, present in all dioceses. However, I would suggest that, as Stadlen's comments on mothering make clear, if clergy do not have a language to articulate much of what they do it will not be easy for them to see these things as important even in a review process. Therefore the current practice of most reviews, which relies almost entirely on the individual clergy assessing and reflecting on their own ministry, is unlikely to offer real insight into all that they do, or don't do, that they may see as unimportant or incidental, even though this might in fact be the bedrock of their efficacy as a parish priest. If they have no language to value it then it is not likely to be shared. It is rare for these reviews to include any element of observation, though there may be anecdotal feedback from parishioners or colleagues. Compared to other professions it seems astonishing that the review process doesn't involve someone external sitting in on a Sunday service, or even some kind of peer observation. Once one is past the stage of a curacy it is rare to receive any kind of feedback on one's ministry, unless specifically requested from a friendly colleague with whom one has shared, or because something has gone really disastrously wrong.

There are in ministry the rewards that come with seeing individuals and congregations flourishing and knowing that the way that you have conducted your ministry has been to some extent instrumental in that flourishing. Yet not all times or congregations or contexts are easy. When things are not going well it can be very hard for clergy because much of what they are doing is difficult to quantify and has no tangible outcomes. In the wider society people are rewarded for their hard work with promotions, pay rises, bonuses and awards. Parish clergy are offered none of these, except promotion for a very few. In the past the 'Easter offering' used to provide some kind of tangible proof of their congregation's estimation of their worth, but such practices are now frowned upon. Many clergy are fortunate in having parishioners who find ways to affirm them and recognize the less tangible skills they utilize. It does seem important, however, that those with the responsibility of care for parish clergy should learn to articulate the many things clergy do, to acknowledge the energy and adaptability that they need and to find ways to make them feel valued for doing what they have been called to do. On a given day in a given parish, much of what a priest does may not look like skilled work, so we need to make sure that those who know its value can find ways to help both that priest and those around them name its worth.

Returning to Stadlen and mothering, we find that she is keen to describe how much mothers have to *learn* in order to mother well. They usually learn quite quickly, because they need to in order to care for the vulnerable child. Seemingly simple processes like comforting a baby need to be learned, and to a certain extent re-learned with any subsequent children. To assume that

144

maternal attributes flow naturally out of the experience of child-birth is to undermine the vast amount of adjustment and learning that is part and parcel of mothering. It is also to fail to acknowledge and affirm when mothers are getting it right. This is practice-based learning. Books and expert advice can be helpful, but mainly offer abstract advice that may or may not work in the concrete reality of this child and this situation. There is a lot of trial and error and a gradual build-up of wisdom acquired through doing mothering. Mothers often find themselves other mothers with whom to develop this wisdom. At toddler groups, the school gates and beyond, women talk about their children and their mothering, looking for affirmation of what is good, shared wisdom in the face of failure, and evidence that others also feel anxious, uncertain or unclear about how best to handle a complex situation. This is often dismissed as women's chat, as if, too, it is nothing special. Increasingly, the pressures of women's work outside the home and different patterns of socializing make these kinds of conversations harder for mothers to participate in. Stadlen would argue that this lack of opportunity for maternal chatting is all part of the problem of not knowing how to talk about and value what it is mothers are doing.

Part of the problem for clergy is that as professionals, paid for their work, they are assumed to be experts. Yet so much of what they do in terms of good parish ministry has to be learned through practice. There are books and courses that provide valuable abstract ideas and advice, but there is plenty of wisdom to be learned through one's own practice and learning from the practice of others. The concrete situations of particular individuals and particular communities require constant adaptability and a certain amount of trial and error. Things that worked in one place might not work in another, simply because the new place is different and requires different handling. In addition there may be few situations where clergy can chat constructively with other practitioners about their work. Traditional working patterns do not create natural opportunities for conversations about daily tasks, and when they do arise insecurity can make it difficult to share honestly. Some of this is down to the very problem of articulation I have tried to highlight. If clergy feel uncertain and insecure about whether or not what they are doing is valuable, then it is hard to talk openly about this. Stadlen says: 'Most of the time, what mothers seem to want from each other is compassion – without advice.'[7]

In seeking to support parish clergy it is important to find ways to listen compassionately to what they are saying, to help them speak of the things they are doing but don't have the language to articulate. The ordinary, practical, getting-on-with-the-job achievements, the intangibility and unquantifiable nature of the valuable work that is being done, need to be acknowledged and championed. Somebody needs to notice and to affirm the faithfulness that keeps on ministering, doing so because as a priest she will do what she can to ensure that those entrusted to her care receive enough to enable them to grow and flourish in their faith.

14
WOMEN, THE CHURCH AND THE WORLD

Elizabeth Loweth

Why did he do it? He knew the roles. What business was it of his trying to change them? Who would it benefit anyway? And what would people say?

Jesus had the temerity actually to speak to a woman in public. He was contravening the rules. He was even treating her as if she were an equal, ready to listen and to be listened to.

He visited with two sisters, different in temperament and in gifts. He spoke with one and dined with the other. Some say that had he been truly hungry, he might have made more favourable remarks about the cook, but the point is, both were important.

He was on his way to respond to the request for help, resulting in the raising of a young girl, when he was touched by a woman with an issue of blood. Not a good scene for a respectable man . . . yet she was healed.

Two thousand years later he is venerated by a Church that struggles to follow his path but somehow misses the mark when it comes to women. How come? Let's look at the situation of women on this planet and then at the North American scene to identify ways in which the Anglican Church might provide support.

Millions of words appear in the worldwide media every day deploring the status of women around the world. The driving

147

force for discrimination against women in almost all circumstances is the achievement of power and control over them. All forms of discrimination and of violence disempower women, even those that are cloaked in the guise of religion. Founders of the major faiths did not advocate mistreatment.

As the Provincial Link for Canada to the International Anglican Women's Network (IAWN), an official network of the Anglican Consultative Council (ACC), I am in communication with other link women who are appointed by their primates, one from each ecclesiastical province. From them comes word of fleeing into the forest to escape armed men, often without knowing which faction of the fighting is pursuing them. Some write about taking in huge numbers of orphaned children and wondering how they can feed them all. Others endure constant fear in repressive regimes where Christians are persecuted, their homes burned to the ground and many killed. Elections bring their own terrors, as competing parties seek to claim victory in political struggles and women dare to vote at their peril. Women suffer brutalities from men who hide behind their own extreme, radical misinterpretations of religious law. Systemic rape has become part of many warring factors. Girls are forbidden to attend school and are victimized if they have the courage to do so. Female infanticide is still prevalent in societies that prefer boys. Health services are too few to serve adequately. Obstetric fistula affects many, and even more are permanently injured through female circumcision. Women who are regarded as the chattel of husbands are found everywhere. Almost all speak of poverty, which is often at the root of other issues.

In spite of all these overwhelming odds, the emails from some of the most challenged and financially deprived areas speak joyously of advances for women within the Church and society. One tells of a 'Magna Carta for Women' to pave the way for equality based on government legislation. Another writes in answer to an IAWN survey about ordained women, that of course they have several and more in the process. From an African country in answer to comments about their achievements to realize ACC 13/31 there is a surprised response that naturally they have equal numbers of women and men on all policy-making units within the Church. In fact the women usually outnumber the men, and what, they wonder, is going on in North America if this is still an issue?

North America – the United States and Canada – may seem carefree and affluent, even cosy in comparison. Yet the Church needs to look again. Societal violence permeates the atmosphere – everything from children's cartoon characters whose pain is supposed to make the audience laugh, to gangs shooting one another simply because they are members of a rival unit. While guns still have some stringent controls in Canada, they are more prevalent in the United States where an amendment to the Constitution gives the right to bear arms within an organized militia.

Drugs remain a scourge of society in every way. Overuse of prescription medications and the illegal use of street drugs both contribute to the erosion of stability. While the first affects only the users and their families, the second too often results in violence to maintain the habit. It can be selling to others, robberies to get cash, attacks on spouses and other individuals, and can lead to homicide and suicide.

Human trafficking is involved in the murders and disappearance of women and girls. Aboriginal women have documented appalling numbers of victims within their population. Men leaving the country to misuse children for their sexual pleasure are too seldom brought to trial on their return, in spite of the laws.

Access to provision of health supports differs between the USA and Canada, the latter having a plan more similar to that of the United Kingdom or Scandinavia. It is a major issue right now in the States, with many interpreting medical coverage with government funding as 'socialism'. It seems difficult for some to realize that tax-supported or assisted medical plans are not unlike tax-supported roads, schools, fire and police protection or sanitation.

Even our language needs examination. 'Adult entertainment' parlours lead the list. It has no link at all to the responsibilities of a mature and adult person. 'Entertainment' is taken to mean watching actually or on film, women or children being exploited.

Tragically they often include child abuse and extreme sexual abuse of women. 'Honour killings' – how can we presume to allow the use of the word honour be so degraded? 'Domestic violence' reduces the violent attack to the dimension of a couple's angry quarrel, or worse, to the discipline of an unruly child. Had the same situation occurred on the street or anywhere else, it would be deemed 'assault', a far more important legal definition. Women, often with the help of their church organizations, have acted on the use and misuse of language in the past. It is time to do so again.

The United Nations Commission on the Status of Women has worked for years to establish the position of women and men as equals and to address some of the major issues affecting women throughout the world. Through the office of the Anglican UN observer, with organization by the staff of the Women's Ministry of the Episcopal Church, and with much funding from AWE (Anglican Women's Empowerment), Anglican women gathered from most of the Communion to attend sessions of the UNCSW. This has been such a successful venture over the past seven years that the Anglican delegation has become the largest registered non-governmental organization present. Much of their work is bearing fruit not only in North America but around the world, through participants who come from the IAWN (International Anglican Women's Network), the Mothers' Union and other Anglican women's organizations. Awareness of the issues, and sharing of ideas and information with the rest of the Church, has proliferated in many ways inside and outside church circles.

This time of gathering in New York has also provided an opportunity for the IAWN Provincial Link women to meet, learn from one another and build the strong network it was created to be. Having been appointed by their primates/presiding bishops, these link women each report directly to the head of their church. It is an awe-inspiring opportunity for change and unity within Anglicanism. One of the most encouraging results of Anglican participation at the UNCSW came at the close of the sessions a couple of years ago. The women, representing most of the 38 ecclesiastical provinces and coming from national churches that were showing signs of division and stress in meeting with other national church leaders, wrote a statement. In it they said that they would not be divided by any single issue, that they would remain solidly together, and that the current disagreement (sexual orientation) would not separate their unity. These women were asking their leaders to unite and identify the real work of the Church rather than utilize precious energy and much-needed resources on divisions. What a powerful position by women deeply involved in the Church and representing the Anglican Communion around the world!

One of the items outlined in instructions for the provincial links is to help establish a women's unit at the national level, and to staff it if none exists. The national office of the Episcopal Church in New York undertook the overall co-ordination of the IAWN and the link women. This huge opportunity for the Anglican Communion was supported by staff who acted as the secretariat with efficiency and care. As of now, that unit of work does not exist as it once did under the former Women's Ministries. The same is true in Canada, where the Women's Desk was dropped some years ago.

While the Church decides through its synods that such support is no longer essential, the secular world is beginning to see women's concerns as pivotal to the human rights agenda at home and abroad. Perhaps the most encouraging very recent development is the establishment of a Council on Women and Girls in the United States. Given a history of very conservative involvement with little financial support for the UN or the UNCSW in the past, this is a major step forward for the US government. President and Michelle Obama are listed at the top of the names bearing primary responsibility for the implementation of the commission's goals. It is a strong commitment, holding out much hope for the future of women in every sense.

The Anglican Church in Canada, like the Episcopal Church in the United States, has an active role to play. Both churches have endorsed Anglican Consultative Council 13/31, a resolution that seeks the equal representation of women and men on the policy-making councils of the Church around the world. Correspondence from our provincial link women in many so-called 'developing nations' speaks of the predominantly large numbers of women within the volunteer councils of the church. At the same time North American statistics, while showing some increase, are not close to achieving the goals of ACC 13/31.

If that level of equality in decision-making should be reached, there would be more attention not only to the needs of women in the Church, but also to their incredible gifts and resources. That in itself would begin to put Anglicans on the path towards more powerfully addressing the issues facing both countries.

At the same time that the government of the USA is taking on unusual responsibility for women's issues, and when the Canadian government is working within its national structures, there is no corresponding office within either national church dealing specifically with women. It is ironic that the national synod in Canada dismantled the Women's Desk some years ago, and just at the time that the federal government was making major advances in women's concerns the Episcopal Church in the United States dismantled its Women's Ministries department. There is much discussion about the reasons. The decisions about programmes and funding are made in both countries by laity, clergy and bishops meeting in national synod or convention. The programmes or staff are assigned in line with the vote on the budget and/or priorities.

It is well known that many, including some women, feel that everything that can or should be done for women has already been accomplished. They overlook issues such as the feminization of poverty, the fact that women are the primary victims of domestic violence, or that the majority of single-parent families are headed by women. There are strong volunteer women's units within both countries, and it is suggested that they can carry the load alone. While that may be, it denies the visible presence within the official national church structures of well over one half of the membership. It makes it much more difficult to focus on specific issues affecting women without staff leadership and responsibility. This does not in any way diminish the impact that remaining staff have on programmes, nor does it reflect any lack of support by church leaders. It does, however, lose that sharp focus that pushed us forward as an ecclesiastical body.

The other looming cloud over the Church is financial. When resources are few, the choices are difficult. Staff may be cut back, further diminishing the public presence of the Church. But there can be another way of looking at it. Women have traditionally been strong financial supporters of church coffers. Whether it is the pennies collected or the huge donations presented by women's groups at diocesan or general conventions or synods, it is the women who have contributed. This is borne out at parish level as well. Given that dimension, it is their money that in part supports everything from the local church roof to the national programme and staff budgets.

For the most part, women's groups are focused on maintaining the pressure on the issues of war, poverty, health, education and violence that strain the bonds of our humanity. How is it, then, that a Church that advocates Millennium Development Goals, including that urging that empowerment of women (#3), has not become actively and visibly involved in working towards that goal by having a specific staffed space for them within its structures?

Internationally women have benefited from the communication of the staff at the Episcopal Church office of Women's Ministries as we share information. That will be greatly missed and it hopefully will be taken over by other staff. It will create a serious gap in communication throughout the Communion.

There is a stark contrast between the advancement reported from around the world by the IAWN links and what is developing in North America. While they report on obtaining a 'women's desk' usually with paid staff, or send along copies of special programmes by the church to enhance women's status, national churches in North America, the area of the world with greatest financial resources, are retrenching.

The loss is enormous, for not only are there specific needs for women, there are well-honed skills and major contributions to the overall work of the Church done exclusively by women. It is they who keep the light shining on the violence of poverty as daily felt by elderly women, or those keeping a family together alone. To a large extent it is women who speak out against the spectres of racism, ageism, sexism, human trafficking, inequality and violence in its multiple forms.

Perhaps the most pervasive form of violence is that of poverty. I call it 'the last surviving form of socially acceptable violence'. That simply means that while the scourges of war, systemic rape, human trafficking and child abuse have been identified as violence and most have been legislated as offensive to society, we still read reports of extreme poverty and somehow our brains categorize it as something that is to be expected – simply a fact of life. It is not. Poverty affects millions around the world including the most affluent countries on earth. It means that from birth, a child lacks the nutrients to grow as God intended. School, if available, becomes more difficult without the right calories to run the brain. Health suffers later in life. Often joblessness occurs when education is not sufficient, and too often the elderly exist with too little food, clothing and shelter. It is an irony that these three – food, clothing and shelter – are defined as basic human necessities, yet are lacked by so many.

The work is enormous. The women in leadership of the Anglican Communion, whether laity, clergy or bishops, will have to take strong positions to move the Church forward – not just for women, but for those whose needs have traditionally been the concern of women.

The women in the Church will, in the end, move forward – but not as easily nor as effectively as they could with support structures and staff. The International Anglican Women's Network will find ways to continue to build a strong web between women in all of the Anglican ecclesiastical provinces. The Mothers' Union will continue to serve families around the world. The Episcopal and Anglican Church Women will work to serve the parishes and outreach programmes. There may even continue to be an Anglican delegation at the UN, though not as representative of the whole Communion. Groups will continue to forward names of capable leaders for church committees at all levels. But the price will be that without some official co-ordination or staff, it will be slower, results will be fewer and the gifts that women bring to the table will be diminished rather than enhanced.

The Gospels reflect the significant role played by women in Jesus' life and ministry. St Paul spoke of the women who enhanced his work in many ways. A diminished place for women within the Church will have an effect on the Anglican Communion around the world.

Every time a woman anywhere is a victim by any cause, she becomes disempowered. How can a Church that advocates ACC 13/31 and MDG #3 possibly move backwards rather than surge forward? Those of us who were privileged to be part of the women in leadership event at Ripon College include many who hold positions of authority within the Church. Together let us work towards the realization of the goal of empowerment of women so that they may continue to serve the Anglican Communion.

15
EPISCOPE AND EISCOPE

Jane Steen

A very attractive lady started attending the services. She started to get friendly with Tristan . . . She was very wealthy and high-class. I told Tristan he would be damned as a toy-boy. But he would not listen. I thought of reporting the matter to the bishop.[1]

The parish priest who is speaking above highlights certain features of episcope that this chapter seeks to address. These include the way in which episcope belongs not only to the bishop but also to the priest, and the way in which it extends beyond the clergy to the well-being of the Christian community, both collectively and individually. Most particularly, however, it indicates how the episcope of the Church is concerned with the kind of outward behaviour that indicates inner quality.

This chapter takes its starting point from this observation. It is written from the perspective of the Church of England, but it is by no means limited to that church. It turns to concepts of character, as these are understood in Stanley Hauerwas's work, to ask what are the inner requirements for those who exercise the complex task of episcope.[2] It suggests that such a role is to be understood not so much in terms of concerns about the exterior functions of oversight, important though these are, but by attention to the interior function of what might be termed *eiscopos*, 'insight'.

In order to make its case, this chapter begins with the ordinals of the Church of England, for it is traditionally in its liturgy that the Church sets out its theology and its ecclesiology. It then turns to biblical descriptions of episcope, before drawing out the implications of both scriptural and liturgical text for questions of character in the exercise of Christian oversight. It concludes with some closing remarks about formation.

The ordinals

The *Book of Common Prayer*, in its ordination rite for bishops, indicates what insight for episcope might entail. Towards the end of the liturgy, the newly ordained bishop is handed a Bible by the archbishop, who says, 'Take heed unto thyself, and to doctrine . . . Be so merciful, that ye be not too remiss; so minister discipline, that you forget not mercy.'[3]

The exercise of episcope has clearly been difficult and demanding for many a long year: mercy and discipline do not always sit easily together. So to prepare for episcope's demands, it is imperative to 'take heed unto thyself'. The verb carries connotations of care and attention, but also of caution and even suspicious attention.[4] Those exercising oversight must be careful concerning their own attentiveness to the Christian life, practising self-scrutiny to equip them for their tasks.

The *Common Worship* ordinal of the Church of England, the contemporary alternative to the *Book of Common Prayer*, offers further comment on the ministry of episcope, and by implication on what is required for its exercise, when it sees it as essentially shared. In the liturgy for the ordination of bishops, the archbishop declares: 'as chief pastors, it is their duty to share with their fellow presbyters the oversight of the Church'.[5]

In the liturgy for the ordination of the presbyters, similarly, the bishop tells the candidates that presbyters 'share with the Bishop in the oversight of the Church, delighting in its beauty and rejoicing in its well-being'.[6]

157

Episcope does not entail individualism, but rather the reverse. This is not to say that the ordinal implies that all responsibility is shared; undoubtedly, different ministries are exercised in different, though not entirely separate, spheres. But it is to emphasize that episcope is required across ministries. As both liturgies go on to remind those to be ordained of their need to 'follow the rule and teaching of our Lord and grow into his likeness', they also suggest the Janus-like nature of oversight: inner regard for oneself is as much a part of episcope as regard for others. Remarks on the nature of oversight in the New Testament confirm this dual perspective.

Biblical episcope

The liturgical instruction in the *Book of Common Prayer* is taken from the book of Acts: 'Take heed therefore unto yourselves, and to all the flock, over the which the Holy Ghost hath made you overseers, to feed the church of God, which he hath purchased with his own blood' (Acts 20.28, KJV). The note of necessity, even urgency, appears again in the letter to the Hebrews: 'See to it [ἐπισκοποῦντες] that no one fails to obtain the grace of God; that no root of bitterness springs up and causes trouble, and through it many become defiled' (Heb. 12.15).[7]

Acts impels those with a clear oversight role to 'take heed', but in the writer of Hebrews, the responsibility for episcope goes further. Hebrews understands the kind of care and attention that go with oversight to belong to the whole community. We see this community responsibility dimension in other texts that highlight the place of attentiveness in episcope, in some texts with almost painful clarity.

Luke and 1 Peter both use 'episcope' to refer to an act rather than a person. The noun may be translated 'visitation', although modern versions often interpret it with additional or alternative words. Luke 19 has Jesus weeping over Jerusalem:

As he came near and saw the city, he wept over it, saying . . . 'They will crush you to the ground, you and your children

158

within you, and they will not leave within you one stone upon another; because you did not recognize the time of your visitation from God.' (Luke 19.41–44)

1 Peter 2.12 offers instruction for Christian living: 'Conduct yourselves honourably among the Gentiles, so that, though they malign you as evildoers, they may see your honourable deeds and glorify God when he comes to judge.'

Luke's Greek lacks 'from God', and has Jesus speaking simply of 'the time of your visitation' [επισκοπη/φ]. Similarly, the Greek text of 1 Peter ρεαδσ δοξα,σωσιν το.ν θεο.ν εϖν η με,ρα| επισκοπη/φ: 'they may glorify God in the day of visitation'. The interpretative history of both verses has varied, but although some modern commentators and translators see visitation in terms of judgement, it also carries positive resonance: a visitation manifests God's power graciously, heralding and even inaugurating the kingdom.[8] As the example of Luke 19 shows, however, those to whom the kingdom is offered must be able to discern it. It is, therefore, of salvific import that the community of the people of God recognize, attend to and receive episcope.

It is arguable that the New Testament itself enables these abilities. Ellen Charry has suggested that the Sermon on the Mount constitutes an aretegenic summary of Jesus' teaching that offers a community identity other than that offered by contemporary Pharisaic Judaism. In the sermon, she suggests, Jesus posits 'hypothetical situations by means of which the disciple can begin to think through what an alternative attitude or behavior would be for any given situation' She goes on to argue:

Jesus is offering an alternative interior purity consisting of a dense concentration of demanding character traits: aggressive self-scrutiny, self-control, compassion, integrity, selflessness and, finally, love of enemies, traits that are essentially limitless in application . . . Jesus' teaching in each case elaborates a basic theme. Disciples are called to rise above self-gratification even when wronged [or] . . . to gratify desire.[9]

159

This vision, this call, which requires not only overseers but all disciples to 'take heed' individually to themselves, has as its outcome the transformed society. It is, perhaps, the insight underlying Hebrews 10.24: considering each other provokes us to love and good deeds because we contemplate in one another the spiritual growth pains we are all experiencing.

This analysis of the Sermon on the Mount suggests that the Christian life is not without internal difficulty; the challenges of discipleship are not all external, provided by opposition and persecution, although such external factors may provide both context and stimulus. Following Jesus involves disciples in their own reformation that will lead them into the likeness of the one whom they imitate. Such likeness is not arrived at by following rules or adhering to codes; it is instead a way of being, consequent upon inner renewal, which, albeit gradually, enables action to cohere with faith as the believer progresses along the path of perfection. Indeed, it might even be said that the ethic of the sermon is an ethic of insight, or interior oversight, requiring self-awareness and self-knowledge in the disciple who seeks to be Christlike.

The scriptural writings offer a picture of care and attention that may appropriately be connected with episcope because of its paradigm in Jesus. 1 Peter 2 employs the image of Jesus the shepherd to describe the saving work of Christ; such imagery is familiar from John, Hebrews and Revelation.[10] 1 Peter 2.25 ends a passage addressed to slaves with Jesus as their shepherd and 'episcopos': 'For you were going astray like sheep, but now you have returned to the shepherd and guardian of your souls.'

Having set the notion of Jesus as shepherd and overseer in the readers' mind, 1 Peter then exhorts leaders to exercise episcope as Jesus did: 'Do not lord it over those in your charge, but be examples to the flock. And when the chief shepherd appears, you will win the crown of glory that never fades away' (1 Pet. 5.3–4). The shepherding of Christ is an example for all Christians, slaves and leaders alike. It is allegiance to the oversight of Jesus, including the living of lives patterned on his, which define the community.[11]

This insistence that Christian identity shapes person and behaviour in the public and social dimension finds common cause with the Pauline corpus. Living thus did not always come easily to the early Church;[12] the contemporary Church should be alert for any blunting of its edges after two thousand years. If it is in attention to Christian identity, and the watchfulness needful for that, that the Church must understand and transfigure its concept of episcope, self-delusion must not prevail. It is entirely possible for any Christian to be in 'a condition in which he can practise self-examination for an hour without discovering any of those facts about himself which are perfectly clear to anyone who has ever lived in the same house with him or worked in the same office'.[13]

Hauerwas pointed out the imperative for a truthful narrative to underlie what he called a community of character.[14] The narrative of the interior life of the individual Christian exercising oversight must be no less truthful.

The character of episcope

Christian character – the acquisition of identity and resultant behaviour – is not the given trait of personality that 'characterizes' an individual in modern parlance. It is rather the formation of the self consequent upon dwelling with God. Such formation is not merely of benefit to the individual. It is made manifest in self-understanding, which determines Christian patterns of living in good times and bad.

Christian character so understood cannot be reduced to abstract moral exhortation. It is entirely dependent on Christ, on Christ's saving work and on the allegiance of the disciple to Christ through faith. Neither, however, can the Christianity that results from this allegiance to Christ be without convicting its adherents to live lives recognizably as described in the Sermon on the Mount. In this sense, the acquisition of Christian character represents one aspect of the search after perfection, or, perhaps in particularly Anglican terms, the quest for holiness, which describes authentic Christian living.

There is some evidence that the exhortation to Christian character was, in the early centuries of the Church, part and parcel of the task of episcope. Gregory the Great begins his *Pastoral Rule* by explaining that he writes of its weighty nature 'in order both that he who is free from them may not unwarily seek them, and that he who has so sought them may tremble for having got them' (p. 1).[15] The Rule insists that interior wisdom is essential to this task of 'the government of souls'. It is, Gregory says, 'the art of arts', for 'who can be ignorant that the sores of the thoughts of men are more occult than the sores of the bowels?' Throughout the book, Gregory offers not simply instruction but spiritual and character-forming discipline to the reader. If this task will be undertaken, certain inner qualities must pertain.

He does not, therefore, mince words when describing the damage done by those who have the role of episcope over others but, lacking what I have termed 'eiscope' concerning themselves, commit such acts as indicate that their inner nature is not compatible with their outer role:

> certainly no one does more harm in the Church than one who has the name and rank of sanctity, while he acts perversely. For him, when he transgresses, no one presumes to take to task; and the offence spreads forcibly for example, when out of reverence to his rank, the sinner is honoured.

Honesty about oneself is an essential aspect of episcope and indeed enables episcope because, as Gregory puts it, everyone 'ought to gather from himself how it behoves him to pity another's weaknesses' (p. 21); it is only insight into one's own heart that enables one to see how often 'vices pass themselves off as virtues' (p. 20).

Gregory's conclusion to the Rule makes it clear that to be in a position of episcope is by no means to be relieved of the necessity or the challenge of increasing in Christian excellence:

> I direct others to the shore of perfection, while myself still tossed among the waves of transgressions. But in the shipwreck

of this present life, sustain me, I beseech thee, by the plank of thy prayer, that, since my own weight sinks me down, the hand of thy merit may raise me up. (p. 72)

Insight must itself be supported by oversight, and Christian character is neither easily acquired nor developed without effort.

The place of character, wisdom and insight in the exercise of episcope raises questions concerning their formation within Christians, and their discernment and cultivation. Screwtape would concur with Gregory on the potential for masquerade, and one must be truly honest about one's own heart to recognize the roots of even virtuous action. Such observations suggest that the responsibility for formation must therefore lie largely with the person seeking that formation. The observation of oneself is essential, more so than observation by others; transfiguration is from within.

However, research has suggested that the most highly regarded aspect of ministerial identity is that of service without regard for recognition; women are, perhaps, particularly attuned to this since, as Janet Soskice has observed, the cooking, cleaning and child-rearing which has traditionally described their lives generally receives little accolade.[16] Moral theology has long taught that *agere sequitur esse*, but the converse is also true: what we do forms who we are.[17] Screwtape may be thwarted by such attention to what is necessary for the execution of the task in hand as governed the composition of Gregory's Rule: it is in doing excellently that we become people of excellence.

Doing that which is required may seem deeply unglamorous. However, Arthur Deikman has drawn attention to the connection between this and the way of the mystic. There is a necessary sidelining of oneself in 'doing what must be done' which works to eliminate at least some of the obstacles that inhibit the 'eiscope' that I have argued is necessary for episcope. If the task requires concentration and effort, it is likely to be conducive to the production of sincerity and humility, for without them it will be partially or ineffectually undertaken. Repeated attention to working in this way, as indeed to the exercise of other virtues of the Christian life, is itself not achieved without attention and self-episcope. As a result, such behaviour is instrumental in the formation of Christian character, and out of Christian character come the resources for Christian oversight as it may be exercised by those who are willing to heed the call of wisdom and 'live, and walk in the way of insight' (Proverbs 9.6).

16

THE EVANGELICAL BURDEN AND IMPERATIVE

Lis Goddard

The whole issue of whether or not women should be consecrated as bishops has in many ways been a defining issue for the evangelical constituency. At a time when the numbers of evangelicals have grown significantly, when there are more evangelical bishops and senior clerics than at any other time, and when the evangelical constituency has become in many ways a major force within the Church, there is a serious question to be asked as to whether evangelicals can engage with each other honestly and creatively. Evangelicals need to do this on the issue not only of scripture's witness regarding women's ministry and leadership and thus of the episcopacy, but also of the nature and scope of episcopal ministry. This latter issue is a discussion that the Church, and in particular evangelicals, has failed to have because it has been so concerned with the issue of whether or not women should be consecrated as bishops. Linked to this, and in many ways creeping up on evangelicals unobserved, is the vitally important question of the implications of what it will mean to have female bishops. There is a very real sense in which evangelicals have not engaged with the need to prepare creatively for this eventuality and I shall examine this as I conclude.

The painful burden of evangelical divisions

It would, of course, be foolish to suggest that the disagreement among evangelicals over women has developed since the consecration of women to the episcopate in the UK became a serious possibility. It was there during the debates leading up to the vote in 1992 on women priests/presbyters. Since then, rather than going away (as some commentators suggested that it would) the division has in fact hardened and served to divide the evangelical constituency still further. It is true that there are some who, upon experiencing the ministry and leadership of women, have been encouraged to re-examine the biblical witness and on doing so have found that things were not as clear-cut as they had thought, or even concluded that there is a strong biblical case to be made for women's leadership. Others, however, upon returning to scripture have found it impossible to change their minds, finding scripture too clear for them on this subject. Still others have returned to scripture with the express intention of fortifying others in their prejudices – whether that be for or against women in leadership and therefore as priests and bishops.

The effect of this upon evangelical Anglicans has been to divide us and to undermine our effectiveness. As a lifelong evangelical, coming from a conservative evangelical home, I have been interested to watch this but also deeply saddened. There are those churches and groups where women and their leadership are clearly welcomed, but they are very separate from those – broadly though not exclusively within the Reform network – where the leadership of women is not welcomed. In the latter, women's *ministry* is broadly encouraged but not women's *leadership*. Sometimes this will mean the ministry of women is restricted to ministry to women and children. The tragedy of recent years has been that rather than working at our differences there has been a tendency to retreat more and more into our respective corners. The effect of this has been a breakdown of our ability of engage effectively in the debates that most affect us. Of course evangelicals are divided by several other issues, such as debates over the atonement, justification and the New Perspective on Paul (in part struggles over whether the definitive interpretation of scripture was given during the Reformation). However, there can be no doubt that the fault line of the differing interpretation of scripture over women's ministry has made it significantly harder for the evangelical constituency to engage constructively with one another. Potentially this is about how we relate to one another, and therefore this issue above all others has destroyed trust.

Given how much evangelicals can disagree over – including issues relating to baptism! – I regularly find myself wondering why we as evangelicals cannot come to a similar place over the biblical testimony regarding women's leadership. For evangelicals this is not simply about culture or justice, nor is it even just about 'gospel values', it is about good exegesis and allowing scripture to form us, to challenge us and to shape us. It is clear to me that a case can be made on both sides of the argument about women's leadership. Even to say that in some quarters is considered anathema, but as a woman struggling with scripture I have to allow for the fact that I could be wrong, and I hope that those who take the other view also allow scripture similarly to challenge them. Nevertheless, I am quite convinced that the case for women in leadership is significantly stronger than that which places limits on women, and that in holding this view I am authentically evangelical. Sadly, this is not something that some of those who disagree with me allow that I might be – as an ordained woman I am not allowed, by my very existence, to be evangelical. Until we can come to scripture and one another with an openness that listens rather than prejudges, we will destroy the very work we most want to do. We are passionate not only about engaging with scripture but also, coming out of that, about preaching the gospel of reconciliation – restoring right relationships, reconciliation between God and humanity and between person and person. We need to reach a place where as evangelicals we can agree to disagree, or go further and accept that this is an issue where we need to acknowledge that scripture can in all honesty be interpreted differently and therefore that there is an inherent call upon us to learn to trust one another. Then we could perhaps begin to do something new and quite remarkable.

It is, I think, noteworthy that the debates in the run-up to the consecration of the first UK women bishops have thus far always been about fear/protection – whether that be for the women who are not yet bishops and who will be bishops[1] or those who could be hurt by the consecration of the women. I understand this and believe in one sense that it is right and proper. However, there is a real need for something more, for some creative thinking. The Church of God should be moving forward, not putting up protective walls.

I am convinced that when God leads his Church forward into a new era, when he challenges her to reform, that reformation will not involve the destruction of part of the Church. Reformation should not involve the alienation and cutting out, like so much dead wood, of part of the Church that is perfectly orthodox, and is indeed alive and kicking. Therefore, the question arises as to what it is that God is doing, what it is that he is asking of us. Are there questions we are not yet asking, things we are not yet doing?

Imagining a new way forward? – transfiguring episcope

I noted earlier that the deep divisions within evangelicalism had prevented the constituency from engaging effectively in the debates that most affect it. By this I meant that evangelicals have allowed themselves to be distracted by their divisions rather than watch for the Spirit and take the initiative in the significant debates surrounding women's ministry and leadership. If evangelicals had been able to think beyond their categories of 'headship' and 'Alpha male' patterns of leadership into trust and a model for accepting each other, they might have been able to have a

168

serious debate about the nature of episcopal leadership instead of only the long-running battle about how to protect themselves from other parts of Christ's body.

What, we need to ask, might a transfigured episcopal ministry look like if we really began to engage with this most fundamental of questions, and how might this enable us to live together?

The prevailing pattern of ministry that has been growing throughout the Church – not simply through expediency but also through careful, convinced theological reflection and study of the scriptures – is a renewed emphasis on every member ministry, on collaborative teamworking, which is flexible and acknowledges and facilitates the gifts of the other. Yet in the episcopate a monarchical structure is still inviolate, justified to an extent by the House of Bishops, which in actual fact still leaves each bishop isolated and, to use a loaded term, 'head' in his own diocese. This is justified by an account of history that fails to engage fully with the political and ideological history of episcopacy, looking only at a particular theological account.

If we are to speak in any sense of an *apostolic* episcopacy it must be not in the sense of institutional continuity, which is passed down and can be 'tainted' by the wrong person being included – how does this fit with the gospel work of the Spirit of Christ in the Church? A more significant and creative conversation to be having in the twenty-first century, which brings us into dialogue with the Reformers, the early Church and our culture, is how our bishops can be truly apostolic in the original, Christocentric sense of the word. That is, how they can be those who are sent to preach the good news of the risen Christ: 'As an apostolic Church the Church can never in any respect be an end in itself, but, following the existence of the apostles, it exists only as it exercises the ministry of a herald.'[2]

It is important (even if controversial) to say that those who are charged with the ministry of oversight are apostolic *only* as they lead in mission. Without this defining ministry the designation is mere form. Here is the question for the Church in the twenty-first century: not, 'Will ordaining women destroy the unity of the Church?', but 'Where does our true unity lie?' Our visible unity

169

is surely not in bishops who may or may not be fulfilling their apostolic mandate, understood as breaking an unbroken male line of headship. If this were so we would be in danger of becoming a Church that is episcocentric rather than Christocentric.

The key question for the Church as we consider women bishops is, 'Can we use this unique moment in the Church's history to transfigure the episcopacy creatively and dynamically so that it becomes a *transfiguring* episcope, a ministry that creatively transfigures the Church into the likeness of Christ and fits her for the apostolic mission to which she is called?'

We need therefore to be asking how our bishops can move from a monarchical, hierarchical, episcocentric model to a collegiate, collaborative apostolic model. Here servant leadership, mutuality and answerability really are at the heart of the oversight offered to us and modelled by those who lead.

If we truly believe that it is good for clergy and laity to work in teams then there should be a move towards colleges of bishops working together. Bishops would be appointed for their skills base, with each diocese served by a team of bishops potentially covering the gifts of Ephesians 4 and leading the people in mission. Thus each diocese would be served by

- an evangelist bishop
- an apostolic bishop – one who oversees church growth, church planting, clergy deployment, and the one who has a real responsibility for strategy
- a pastor bishop
- a prophetic bishop – the preacher/teacher with the training portfolio (not just a trainer but someone with a clearly prophetic gift).[3]

This would have a variety of effects. It would create bigger dioceses and so fewer diocesan structures, as already happens where dioceses are beginning to share diocesan officers, as in Coventry and Sheffield, thus saving money for the task of ministry. It would also open up new ways of doing it because of the new truly collegiate nature of the episcopal ministry. There could be part-time bishops, job-sharing bishops and the possibility of maternity/paternity leave. Being a bishop could become something that more women were willing to do, rather than fear that it was something that swallowed you whole.[4] Such a transfigured episcopacy could, very importantly, provide for a bishop within the diocesan college to have and actively exercise the cure of souls among the clergy, someone who specifically pastored them – even while another colleague was perhaps overseeing a clergy discipline measure. Pastoral care, that is, the role of the bishop as shepherd, as well as truly apostolic, missional ministry, would be restored to the heart of the episcopate. Episcope would be transfigured into what it was always meant to be, making it fit for purpose for the twenty-first century.

One of the other exciting side-effects of this reimagining is that it has the potential to enable those who disagree about women's ministry to work side by side in the episcopate. I am very aware that for many this is simply impossible because of their understanding of the nature of the unity of the Church and their unwillingness/inability to recognize women's orders. If, however, we were willing to do some serious work re-examining the basis of our unity rather than just accept the view that our unity is focused in the bishop as the essentially Anglican line, then we might perhaps be able to move forward creatively. I am not suggesting that it would be easy, but proposing another way that might help us to begin to think in new ways that make space for one another. It might allow us not only to discover a new way to understand the unity of the Church but also of how we can understand what it is to be a bishop and to relate to those in authority. We could have a college of bishops working together in a diocese, and in each college there would always be at least one bishop of each integrity to preserve the balance within the diocese. All would agree to work together not because they deny their differences but rather acknowledge them under the Lordship of Christ, bound by his word, held in unity by him and sent out in common mission by him.

This is a model that other professions employ.[5] Bishops could share taking the chair, such a role not assuming any sort of hierarchy or headship as there would be a collegiate responsibility. Bishops serve a Church that teaches collaborative leadership and worships the triune God who in Christ took the form of a slave for us (Phil. 2.6), and enjoins us that 'whoever wishes to be great among you must be your servant, and whoever wishes to be first must be the slave of all. For the Son of Man came not to be served but to serve, and to give his life as a ransom for many' (Mark 10.43–44). This pattern must supremely apply to bishops, given that Peter describes Christ himself as the one 'bishop of our souls' (1 Pet. 2.25). Our tradition of monoepiscopacy and prelacy appears to run counter to this gospel vision.

Although much more could be said about how the theology and ministry of the episcope could be reimagined, this chapter would not be complete without looking at another important challenge that the transfiguring of the episcope poses for the evangelical wing of the Church in particular, but is not being faced.

Evangelicals and women in senior leadership

In the introductory booklet to the Transfiguring Episcope conference, the authors wrote: 'We hope to identify the qualities, skills, experience and training needed to equip women to thrive in leadership.'[6] At the time that struck me as a key issue that the Church needs to address. I have become increasingly convinced that this is particularly important for the evangelical wing of the Church. Following the conference my overwhelming impression was of how far behind evangelicals are in the nurturing of their women for leadership, particularly potential episcopal leadership.

It was interesting to note, looking down the list of conference attendees, how many were in posts that have traditionally been considered 'senior' posts by those within the church hierarchy: deans, archdeacons, canons, those in theological education or college chaplains, bishop's chaplains, on bishop's senior staff as

DDOs or deans of women ministry (I write as someone who has been both a chaplain of an Oxford College and taught at a theological college). It would, of course, make sense to invite such women to a conference looking at the episcopacy and women's future role within it. When the Church of England does decide to consecrate women bishops it is very likely that the first appointments will be from among this group of 'senior' women. What struck me, however, and other evangelicals who were there, was just how comparatively few evangelicals there were among our number.

The reason for this paucity of evangelicals seems fairly straightforward. Seniority in the evangelical wing of the Church is not generally understood in the same way as within the rest of the Church. For evangelicals it is the leaders of the large and successful churches, the speakers on the main stages at the big conventions, like Spring Harvest, New Wine, Word Alive and NEAC, who have seniority. These are the evangelical Anglicans who effectively have a ministry of oversight, of episcope.[7] Traditionally, most evangelicals are uninterested in 'preferment' in the traditional sense and are often suspicious of those among their number who pursue a 'career path' or who too actively display ambition for a 'purple shirt'.

Given this situation, it is vital to reflect upon the dearth of evangelical women in the so-called senior posts both within the hierarchy of the Church and within evangelicalism itself. Evangelical women, like their male evangelical counterparts traditionally, are, in my observation, unlikely to apply for the traditional 'senior posts'. They often see them as taking them away from the real task in hand. When I was Chaplain of Jesus College in Oxford I was very much in the minority as an evangelical among my colleagues, and as a female evangelical I was in a minority of one. In contrast, I regularly meet, through my work with AWE-SOME,[8] evangelical women who are involved in Fresh Expressions, at the forefront of mission initiatives, leading growing inner-city and rural churches, doing outreach in exciting sector ministry and leading team ministries and medium-sized churches. I have often had the question put to me by evangelical women in typically activist terms: why would I want to sit on lots of committees when I could be getting on with the job?

If the fact that evangelical women are not attracted to the traditional senior posts is part of the problem, the additional challenge is that the evangelical wing of the Church is not actively encouraging its key women. In fact, it could be said to be actively discouraging them. I constantly hear stories from other women of interview processes that have inexplicably gone against them. I hear these stories from deans of women's ministries who tell me that they cannot understand why gifted women are blocked by evangelical churches who say they value women's ministry and yet then appoint less able or less well-qualified men. This often leads to these women taking jobs outside the evangelical fold. There is, of course, nothing wrong in going outside the evangelical fold, indeed it is laudable and important for gifted women to be willing to go anywhere and to grow churches where they are needed. It cannot, however, be denied that such a move does have implications among some evangelicals. It is very easy to be labelled as no longer 'one of us', especially if one is female and therefore a little suspect already.

One also rarely sees an ordained woman speaking on the main stage at one of the big evangelical events, and this is in part because to do this one needs to be leading a 'known'/recognizable church or community. The spouses of male church leaders will speak and other lay women are invited, but I have lost count of the number of times I have been told by evangelicals that there are no gifted women speakers who are ordained. I sometimes wonder what happens so that gifted lay evangelical women lose their teaching and preaching ability when they are theologically trained and commissioned by the Church!

The reality is that the 'career ladder' for evangelicals is generally different from that of the rest of the Church, but I do not think that this is recognized widely. The truth is that a woman needs to do much more to 'progress' on it than a man does, and much more experience is asked of her than of her male counterparts. Whereas a man will often find that he is shortlisted for big jobs early on, a woman will need to have done several jobs before she can expect to be taken seriously, and then she may be considered too old! Where men are regularly mentored, women are not. I think of one large church that sent several ordinands to the same theological college. The vicar was faithful in visiting them and spending time with them. However, it quickly became clear that he visited only the men and never the female ordinand his church had sent, and no one else came to mentor and support her. Similarly, where male ordinands leaving theological college find networks working for them, women rarely do. Evangelical churches also do not see the need to provide good, strong ordained female role models for their young women, or the need to encourage women into the ordained ministry. I think of one very large church in London, which is in theory supportive of women's ministry, that recruits at least one new ordained staff member a year, and yet still has not had one ordained woman on its staff.

All of this is important because the truth is that unless you have been trained in the right place, done the right curacy and had the right sort of first appointment, it is very hard to secure certain evangelical posts, to be recognized within the constituency. Until these things are addressed, evangelical women will continue to face serious problems in terms of appointments. And the evangelical constituency will not have faced up to its collective failure towards its women leaders, both those currently serving and those who should be being nurtured for the future. Evangelicals need to think seriously about how we respond to this challenge, how we nurture our able women so that they too are ready to take their place alongside their male counterparts and their female colleagues from other wings of the Church.

Conclusion

As the Church of England looks towards consecrating women as bishops, there are serious questions to be asked about how as a Church we learn to live together. It would be all too easy to decide to make a change that effectively breaks entirely with the past. I would argue that there is an onus on evangelicals not to do this but to find a way to engage with one another and with scripture. This means not only finding a way to live with those with whom we disagree, but also encouraging and developing the young women in our midst with real leadership gift.

Alongside this there is the vital question that faces the whole Church, which we will need to face sooner or later, of what kind of episcopacy we want to have. We can either take the initiative and address that now, when we are facing key questions about the nature of our unity and identity, or we can duck it and wait (as we did with the question of priests) until it is forced upon us by pragmatic considerations occasioned by finance and the realities of the needs of women in the episcopacy.

Ours is a gospel of grace, the grace that transforms. This is surely a time in the Church's history when we are being called by the Spirit to be part of his transforming action.

CLOSING REFLECTION

Katharine Jefferts Schori

'Stir up your might, O Lord, and come to save us. Restore us, let your face shine, that we may be saved.' I imagine that prayer has been said many times. And perhaps even more often the prayer, 'How long, O Lord, how long?'

Well, stir up your courage, my sisters and brothers. God is at work, even when you can't see the seed growing or hear the angel speaking in the night. The faithfulness you need in order to endure comes from God. This struggle is not new, yet you are soon to be delivered – soon enough, in God's time. Those who endure to the end will be saved.

There is plenty of fear around here and around the Anglican Communion just now – don't let it be yours. Jesus may say, 'Don't worry about how you're going to speak or what you're going to say', but the BBC wanted my sermon texts for Sunday ten days ahead of time! My reply was, 'The Spirit isn't working quite that far ahead of time.' 'Well, we are responsible for every word that goes out over these broadcasts . . .' Fear seems to be equal opportunity, free floating, not just here, but almost anywhere there are human beings struggling with truth and their take on ultimate meaning.

'I'm sending you out like sheep into the midst of wolves, so be wise as serpents and innocent as doves.' Are you or we sheep among the wolves? And if so, does being a sheep mean rolling

177

over and playing dead? Well, what gifts do sheep have? Wool, lots of it at the right time of the year – that might just stick in a wolf's throat if it's long enough. And if a whole bunch of sheep get together, they can defend themselves against a wolf, even pretty aggressively. But I don't think Jesus is encouraging striking the wolf with hooves or butting it to death. It's that ability to get together that is the greatest gift the sheep have – that herding instinct that can put the weakest in the centre and gather round them. Don't put anybody out there all alone.

Sheep can survive on pretty meagre grazing; goats are even better at it, but most of the biblical writers have a pretty dim view of goats – they're seen as too smart for their own good, most of the time. But sheep can find food, and even thrive, in places that look a lot like a desert. How is this flock going to keep finding adequate grazing, and support each other in the process? Who are the shepherds who are going to keep the flock moving between oases? Sheep – care for your shepherds. Shepherds – tend your flocks.

Who or what are the wolves? I'm not so sure it's our opponents. I think the wolves have a lot more to do with what we fear most – and most of that is internal. The wolves don't get the upper hand unless the sheep are not paying attention to the shepherd – unless they've scattered. Wolves have to find prey to survive; sheep don't have to co-operate. That take on things sometimes looks like what the Canon to the Ordinary in Nevada used to call 'malicious compliance' (or 'subversive overcompliance)'. It underlies all of Jesus' language about walking the extra mile (to catch the soldier off guard) and giving away your coat, and turning the other cheek, so the hitter has to recognize you equally as a human being.

Be wise as serpents – lie there in the sun, looking lazy, taking in everything that's going on. Listen to the vibrations of marchers far away, notice the odours of fear, sense the heat of those advancing, and take to your holes when you have to. And be innocent as doves – like Jesus, go around unprotected by the violent response to fear. Fly above it.

What if all the women clergy of the Church of England took a Sunday off? What would happen if they and all their supporters

178

stayed away? Do you think the Church would notice? A CNN reporter noticed something quite interesting this week. He said, 'Well, 1,300 clergy may have said they're leaving the C of E if it consents to women bishops, but I couldn't find anybody at the Synod who would say why. There was no representative of that position anywhere to be found.' Sometimes the doves get above the fray, and ask the awkward questions.

Maybe you know the story of the women of the Niger delta. Oil exploitation in that part of the world has devastated villages, poisoned the drinking water and the fish by spilling crude oil. The flares that burn off excess gas pollute the atmosphere and cover everything with soot. The villagers worked for years to get the oil companies to change their habits. They were in a bind, for they had nowhere else to go, and they had long depended on the fruits of the earth and sea to survive. They pleaded and picketed, and some even tried destroying the pipes and machinery. Nothing worked. Finally a large group of women marched down to the corporate offices, sat down outside the building, and took off their shirts. They didn't shame themselves; in that culture they shamed anyone who saw them, and they shamed their opposition into action. The oil companies began to negotiate.

Doves can fly above the armies gathering, and spend their energy where it will do most good. They can't do much to defend themselves on the ground; their safety lies in a larger perspective. Wise as serpents, innocent as doves. We've just watched Ingrid Betancourt and several other hostages delivered from years of captivity in the jungles of Colombia. If what we saw was accurate, it was a pretty wily operation, that somehow managed to avoid violence – only by the grace of God. I'm not convinced that they would not have resorted to violence if something had gone wrong, but it is the kind of crafty wisdom for which snakes are known. Wilier yet if it was a ransom operation.

Ingrid and her fellow captives endured years in the jungle, feeling pretty despondent. Come and save us, O Lord. Who else tells a story like that – lost, misunderstood, abandoned? Hagar's story is like that, and others who read her story remember that she and her offspring also got a blessing and promise from God.

179

The woman at the well certainly is a witness to that kind of endurance. So was Hildegard and the other mystic women of the Middle Ages. You walk in the footsteps of the wise women burned at the stake for being uppity enough to think that they could heal people. Your witness and solidarity mean that you hold the hands of the trafficked and the abandoned ones. Your preaching can speak the pain and injustice of women and girls mutilated or married too young 'for cultural reasons' and women of all ages raped by the doers of war. And you are also the sister of the 41-year-old mother who made the Olympic swimming team in four events – Dara Torres may seem as strong as the teenagers, though not for long, but she is far wiser.

You are building that vision Hosea speaks of: Israel blossoming like the lily, and abundant as the forests of Lebanon – a community fruitful and fragrant, flourishing with abundance for a feast. Keep nourishing that vision, not with the warrior's tools, but with the wiliest and most challenging creations of the spirit you can muster. Those who endure will ultimately be blessed.

APPENDIX I
2009 CLERGY COMPENSATION REPORT—GENDER STATISTICS[*]

Table 1: Full-time compensation by gender and position in comparative perspective

ALL CLERGY — Parochial and non-parochial

Gender	Median	No.	% of Total N
Male	$71,859	3817	66.6%
Female	$61,519	1914	33.4%
Total	$67,820	5731	100.0%

SENIOR CLERGY

Gender	Median	No.	% of Total N
Male	$98,043	650	82.1%
Female	$83,516	142	17.9%
Total	$94,942	792	100.0%

SOLO CLERGY

Gender	Median	No.	% of Total N
Male	$66,539	2276	66.5%
Female	$59,113	1144	33.5%
Total	$64,483	3420	100.0%

ASSOCIATES, ASSISTANTS AND CURATES

Gender	Median	No.	% of Total N
Male	$57,042	518	47.0%
Female	$53,612	584	53.0%
Total	$55,000	1102	100.0%

SPECIALIST MINISTERS

Gender	Median	No.	% of Total N
Male	$67,906	537	62.2%
Female	$58,234	326	37.8%
Total	$64,000	863	100.0%

---

[*]Matthew Price, "2009 Episcopal Church Compensation Report." Department of Analytical Research, Church Pension Group, New York. See full report at http://download.cpg.org/home/publications/pdf/2009_Compensation_Report.pdf.

Table 2: Clergy compensation by years of experience		
Gender	Years credited service / Episcopal job experience	Median clergy compensation
Male	1 to 5 Yrs	$56,295
	5 to 10 Yrs	$67,334
	10 to 20 Yrs	$74,448
	20 Years Plus	$84,679
	Total	$72,015
Female	1 to 5 Yrs	$53,458
	5 to 10 Yrs	$60,452
	10 to 20 Yrs	$68,085
	20 Years Plus	$73,230
	Total	$61,618
Total	1 to 5 Yrs	$54,984
	5 to 10 Yrs	$64,479
	10 to 20 Yrs	$71,980
	20 Years Plus	$82,850
	Total	$68,040

Table 3: Clergy compensation by age				
Gender	Age of cleric	Median compensation	Number of clergy	Percentage of clergy
Male	18 to 35	$57,748	282	7.4%
	35 to 45	$68,237	529	13.9%
	45 to 55	$73,676	1139	29.8%
	Over 55	$74,984	1867	48.9%
	Total	$71,859	3817	100.0%
Female	18 to 35	$54,040	143	7.5%
	35 to 45	$60,712	226	11.8%
	45 to 55	$62,885	591	30.9%
	Over 55	$62,738	954	49.8%
	Total	$61,519	1914	100.0%
Total	18 to 35	$55,770	425	7.4%
	35 to 45	$66,000	755	13.2%
	45 to 55	$69,972	1730	30.2%
	Over 55	$70,000	2821	49.2%
	Total	$67,820	5731	100.0%

Table 4: Median compensation by rank and gender				
Gender	Province	Senior clergy	Solo clergy	Associates and curates
Male	I	$99,603	$73,865	$60,000
	II	$110,739	$71,997	$57,257
	III	$103,682	$69,250	$57,801
	IV	$100,682	$66,401	$58,358
	V	$85,500	$61,165	$54,588
	VI	$80,750	$62,750	$38,500
	VII	$97,763	$62,459	$60,000
	VIII	$89,961	$65,255	$54,600
	Total	**$98,043**	**$66,539**	**$57,042**
Female	I	$83,958	$63,938	$54,489
	II	$87,565	$62,884	$54,127
	III	$89,592	$62,926	$58,019
	IV	$74,079	$55,368	$52,376
	V	$88,484	$56,482	$54,600
	VI	$75,000	$53,141	$37,950
	VII	$85,505	$56,571	$52,000
	VIII	$84,167	$60,000	$53,500
	Total	**$83,516**	**$59,113**	**$53,612**
All Clergy	I	$94,123	$67,776	$55,161
	II	$109,295	$69,129	$55,731
	III	$99,821	$67,089	$57,882
	IV	$97,596	$63,954	$55,151
	V	$85,500	$59,425	$54,600
	VI	$77,000	$58,921	$37,950
	VII	$95,405	$59,414	$55,758
	VIII	$88,465	$63,414	$53,740
	Total	$94,942	$64,484	$55,000

APPENDIX 2
2006 STATE OF THE CLERGY REPORT—GENDER STATISTICS AND ANALYSIS*

There are striking differences in the numbers of men and women ordained by Province with significant gender differences in Provinces IV and VII which make up the bulk of the geographically Southern dioceses. (This same data can be seen in map form on Map One: Gender Differences in Numbers Ordained, 2003 through 2005). This pattern is significant when

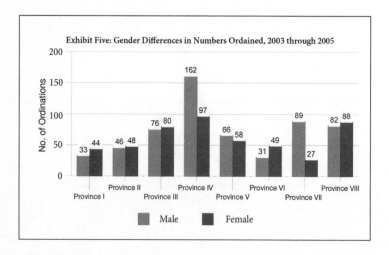

Exhibit Five: Gender Differences in Numbers Ordained, 2003 through 2005

---

*Matthew Price, "2006 State of the Clergy Report." Department of Analytical Research, Church Pension Group, New York. See full report at http://download.cpg.org/home/publications/pdf/stateofclergy2006.pdf.

184

seen in light of a trend towards younger male ordinands in some regions. Exhibit Six shows that in Provinces I and VII, the median age at ordination for men has fallen below 40, a significant milestone in terms of a statistical indicator. It also demonstrates that there has not been as much success in recruiting

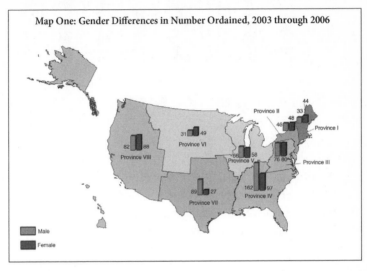

Map One: Gender Differences in Number Ordained, 2003 through 2006

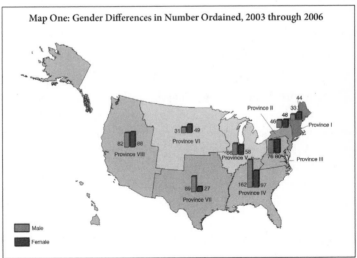

Map One: Gender Differences in Number Ordained, 2003 through 2006

185

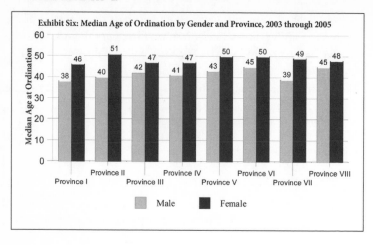

Exhibit Six: Median Age of Ordination by Gender and Province, 2003 through 2005

younger females to the ordination process as there has been with younger males. An even more striking sense of the regional pattern of these gender differences can be seen in Map Two where the percentage of those ordained under 35 varies significantly by gender.

Section Two: Clergy Careers Stage One, New Ordinands and Employment

Despite regionally based gender differences in patterns of ordination, both the overall numbers of those being ordained, and those ordinands who become active in the Church, are fairly close to being in balance. Looking at Exhibit Seven, it is clear that the gender balance of the Church does look set to change, even if the age structure does not. There is a significant difference between new entrants to the pool of those actively employed within the Church and those retiring. We expect the trend toward a more evenly balanced gender profile for active clergy to continue. It should be noted that women ordinands find employment in a first job in roughly the same proportions

**Exhibit Seven: Newly Ordained Clergy 2003-2005,
Clergy Retiring 2003-2005, and Currently Active Clergy by Gender**

Gender	Ordained to Priesthood	New Ordinands Now Employed	Newly Retired	Active Clergy
Male	54%	53%	85%	69%
Female	46%	47%	15%	31%

as men, with two-thirds of those ordained ending up employed in the Church.

While the probability of employment is roughly equal in terms of gender, the same could not be said of age. Exhibit Eight shows the percentage of the 2003–2005 ordinands who are currently employed in the Church. The most likely group to find employment in the Church are women under the age of 35 with 81% being employed. Employment percentages decline significantly for men over 45 and women over 55 and are lowest of all for men over 55 with just 38% of such men finding employment in the Church.

**Exhibit Eight: Employment by
Age at Ordination, 2003 through 2005**

Age at Ordination	Male	Female
25-35	77%	81%
35-45	78%	71%
45-55	59%	72%
55 plus	38%	46%
Total	66%	67%

Not only does a combination of age and gender influence the probability of employment, it also influences what type of positions new ordinands get in parishes. As can be seen in Exhibits Nine and Ten, which look at the proportions of those who are associates or curates versus solo rectors, by far the most likely course for younger ordinands is to be placed in associate, assistant or curate positions, with almost 90% of women ordinands under 35 and 71% of similarly aged males being employed in such positions. By contrast, 45% of female ordinands who are over the age of 55 are solo rectors and two-thirds of males over 55 occupy such positions. One might argue that sole charge of a parish is a position of greater responsibility than an assisting clergy role, but Exhibit Eleven shows this assumption would not be reflected in median compensation levels of clergy by age. In fact, the younger clergy, who are most likely to be assisting rather than in charge, receive the highest level of compensation.

It is also interesting that the highest-earning group in the exhibit are women under age 35, although the median compensation level for women ordinands overall is slightly lower than for men. As we see in the next section, when looking at the compensation levels of all clergy, there is a significant and persistent gender gap in compensation.

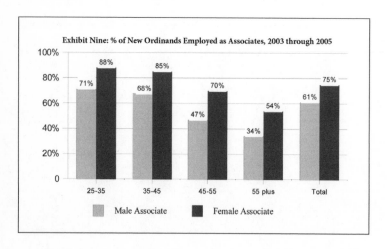

Exhibit Nine: % of New Ordinands Employed as Associates, 2003 through 2005

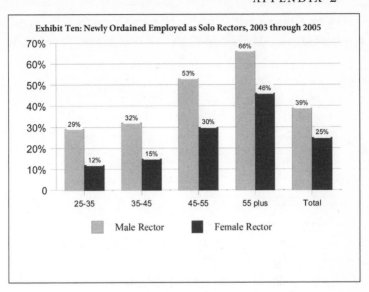

Exhibit Ten: Newly Ordained Employed as Solo Rectors, 2003 through 2005

Exhibit Eleven: Compensation by Age and Gender for Those Ordained 2003 through 2005			
Age at Ordination	Compensation All New Ordinands	Compensation New Male Ordinands	Compensation New Female Ordinands
25-35	$47,669	$46,916	$48,318
35-45	$46,578	$48,050	$45,432
45-55	$45,115	$47,295	$43,186
55 plus	$38,839	$43,643	$33,547
Total	$45,922	$47,056	$45,000

Section Three: The Pay Gap, and Gender Patterns in Clergy Careers

In Exhibit Twelve, we can see there is a large overall gap in compensation levels for clergy men and women. On average, full-time male clergy earn 17.5% more than full-time women clergy, defining full time as earning over $27,000. In 2001, when we first started publishing differences in compensation by

Exhibit Twelve: Compensation by Gender and Position for Currently Active Clergy			
Cleric's Job Level	Gender	% of Total	Median Comp.
All Full Time Clergy	Male	71.3%	$64,825
	Female	28.7%	$55,076
	Total	100.0%	$61,379
Associate or Curate	Male	50.1%	$56,536
	Female	49.9%	$51,610
	Total	100.0%	$53,500
Senior Rector *(In charge of a multi-clergy congregation)*	Male	85.6%	$86,137
	Female	14.4%	$74,166
	Total	100.0%	$83,425
Solo Rector *(The sole cleric responsible for the congregation)*	Male	74.2%	$60,822
	Female	25.8%	$55,511
	Total	100.0%	$59,532
Non-Parochial	Male	70.9%	$68,117
	Female	29.1%	$56,431
	Total	100.0%	$64,002

gender, male clergy earned $57,369 and female clergy $48,645, an 18% gap; hence the progress toward compensation equity is slow. As can also be seen from Exhibit Twelve, the pay gap still exists even when comparing men and women in the same relative positions.

The gender gap is also not explained by men having more years of credited service. As can be seen in Exhibit Thirteen, with more years of credited service, the gap between male and female median compensation grows. Some of the initial theories we had as to why this gap occurred have not been borne out by the data.

Believing that gaps in service might be having a detrimental effect on women's clerical careers we looked to see if men and women differed overall in the number of years they have been ordained and years of credited service. On average, there does not seem to be a significant difference, although further research will be needed to see if we find particular patterns as to when men and women have gaps in service and for what reasons. Another line of analysis we pursued was to see if female clergy were more likely to drop out of active service in comparison to males. In our analysis, we found that, with the exception of the last four years, female clergy are less likely to be have become actively employed, this being true of 28% of women clergy as against 18% of men. But once they are employed, women clergy don't seem any more likely to drop out of active service than male clergy. Of all the non-retired clergy for whom we have

Exhibit Thirteen: Compensation for Full-Time Clergy by Years of Credited Service and Gender			
Credited Service	Cleric's Total Compensation All Clergy	Total Compensation Male Clergy	Total Compensation Female Clergy
1 to 5 yrs	$50,129	$51,017	$48,498
5 to 10 yrs	$58,195	$59,740	$55,978
10 to 20 yrs	$64,214	$66,516	$60,386
Over 20 yrs	$73,193	$73,626	$65,101

employment histories, approximately 75% are still active, and this is true for those who start in both parochial and non-parochial situations.

One clue to the compensation gender gap may be the particular career patterns that female and male clergy careers appear to follow. Exhibits Fourteen and Fifteen show the distribution of parish positions by gender and years of credited service for active male and female clergy.

Comparing the two exhibits is informative. The proportion of female clergy who occupy some type of assisting clergy role not only larger at the outset compared to men—42% for men versus 59% for women—but remains higher even at the upper end of the credited service range. Thus, while only 5% of men are in associate, assistant, or curate roles after 20 years, this is true for 16% of female clergy. By contrast, the proportion of women clergy occupying senior rector positions grows more slowly than that of males and thus while after 10 years of credited service almost one quarter of male clergy have achieved the position of senior rector, this is true for just 13% of women clergy. If we

Exhibit Fourteen: Parish Position by Service, Male Clergy

Years of Credited Service

Senior Rector Solo Rector
Associate or Curate

Exhibit Fifteen: Parish Position by Service, Female Clergy

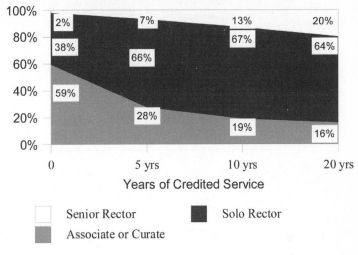

then look at the congregations that women are in when they become solo rectors we can gain a greater understanding, perhaps, both as to why women remain in assisting roles and the compensation gap between men and women.

Exhibit Sixteen shows that when women are in sole clergy positions, they are in charge of congregations with lower Average Sunday Attendance (ASA) and Operating Revenues than is the case with male clergy and this is true regardless of years of Credited Service.**

With Average Sunday Attendance and Operating Revenue lower for the congregations in which women have sole charge, it is hardly surprising that women have a tendency to serve in assisting clergy positions. Moreover, this may help explain why the 2001 Pulpit and Pew study found that female rectors suffered

---

**The Average Sunday Attendance and Operating Revenue figures come from the 2004 Parochial Report. CPG would like to thank Dr. Kirk Hadaway and the Office of Research and Statistics at the Church Center for providing access to this data made possible by the collaborative relationship that now exists between our two organizations in the standardization and exchange of data.

Exhibit Sixteen: Attendance and Revenue Congregations and Solo Rectors by Gender and Credited Service

		ASA	Operating Revenue
All Solo Rectors	Male	124	$220,963
	Female	95	$177,407
	Total	116	$209,712
1 to 5 yrs Credited Service	Male	92	$171,019
	Female	81	$157,842
	Total	88	$166,538
5 to 10 yrs Credited Service	Male	115	$196,752
	Female	88	$159,025
	Total	105	$182,482
10 to 20 yrs Credited Service	Male	126	$222,804
	Female	106	$195,654
	Total	120	$214,224
Over 20 yrs Credited Service	Male	137	$249,143
	Female	103	$201,784
	Total	135	$245,630

more highly from stress than male rectors. If female rectors are either having as their first cure the rectorship of a congregation that is relatively under-resourced, or if they are moving from multi-clergy congregations that are well resourced to ones with more constrained finances, this would almost certainly heighten stress levels. While it does not seem from our analysis of the parish clergy "drop out" problem that women in the parish are actually leaving in higher numbers, there are certainly the factors present that would increase levels of stress.

A brief case study of clergy men and women in the Diocese of Maryland seems to indicate that there is a difference in the types of cures with which women and men begin their careers, with women having a higher proportion of associate or curate positions than men. In addition, men are more likely to work in a non-parochial setting, which may slightly inflate salary, especially in diocesan positions. The reason for this difference is not clear, but may be partially affected by the start date of the different genders' careers. Men, in general, began their careers in the Church earlier than women and tend to have longer work histories. Women were much more likely to postpone ordination until after their children were grown, while men showed no specific preference with regard to children's ages. While women do receive some solo and senior rector positions upon ordination, their start dates tend to be restricted to the last 10 years, whereas men's start dates span the past 40. This may account for some of the perceived difference in the treatment of men and women in the Church with regard to employment opportunities.

Further analysis of clergy women's careers is clearly necessary, but we can see that clergy women are far more likely to start and remain in assisting clergy positions. Such positions clearly have advantages, including the possibility of strong mentoring relationships with an experienced rector. Associate or curate positions may also offer more flexibility simply because multi-clergy congregations allow clergy to cover for each other when unexpected commitments and emergencies arise. But such positions may potentially make the transition to being in sole charge that much more difficult, especially if the sole charge congregation is constrained in its resources. We hope that with further research, we can assist the larger Church, dioceses, and parishes to gain additional insight and formulate solutions to these problems.

NOTES

Introduction

1 First a word of background. My involvement in the conference was largely due to my role and work in the Anglican Communion. I am Director for Theological Studies in the Anglican Communion Office. In this capacity I have acted as Secretary to the Working Party on Theological Education (TEAC) established by the Anglican Primates in 2002. At a meeting of TEAC in Singapore in May 2007 we produced a document, 'The Anglican Way: Signposts on a Common Journey', which endeavoured to set out in a succinct form the essentials of the 'Anglican Way', particularly bearing the needs of ministerial theological education in mind (the Signposts statement itself can be found online at http://www.anglicancommunion. org/ministry/theological/signposts/english.cfm). This Signposts statement, which then provided the key resource for the exploration of Anglican identity by the bishops at the 2008 Lambeth Conference, is divided into four sections, headed respectively, 'Formed by Scripture', 'Shaped through Worship', 'Ordered for Communion', 'Directed by God's Mission'. One of the features of the statement is that there is an implicit flow, so that one section leads into the next. However, 'Mission' is both the goal of the document and also its underpinning. Shortly after the Singapore meeting I wrote an article about the Signposts statement which appeared in the journal *Anglican World*. In that article I drew connections between the different sections of the statement and the biblical motif of transfiguration (that article can be found online at http://www.anglicancommunion.org/resources/aw/downloads/126/aw126b.pdf and http://www.anglicancommunion.org/resources/aw/downloads/126/aw126c.pdf).

In what I write here I draw on those earlier comments, but my current reflections are focused more specifically on 'episcope'.

2 Michael Ramsey, *The Glory of God and the Transfiguration of Christ* (London: DLT, 1949 pb 1967), p. 144.

3 See Walter Brueggemann, 'Trajectories in Old Testament Literature and the Sociology of Ancient Israel', *JBL* 98, 1979, for the concept of strands or trajectories existing in a creative tension.

196

4 There are other small differences in Matthew's account compared with Mark – the reference to Jesus' face, the mention of the cloud and the changed order in referring to Moses and Elijah. These differences are further emphasized in Luke's account, discussed below.

1 Follow Who?

1 Accessed 7 July 2009.

2 All biblical quotations are taken from Nicholas King SJ, *The New Testament Freshly Translated* (Stowmarket: Kevin Mayhew, 2004).

3 An extensive study of women in Mark's Gospel may be found in Susan Miller, *Women in Mark's Gospel* (Edinburgh: T & T Clark, 2004).

4 An eleventh-century prayer of St Anselm translated by Benedicta Ward in *The Prayers and Meditations of Saint Anselm* (Penguin Classics, 1973), p. 152.

5 B. R. Gaventa, *Our Mother Saint Paul* (Westminster John Knox, 2007).

2 How did Jesus Develop Women as Leaders?

1 J. Lawrence, *Growing Leaders* (BRF/CPAS, 2004), p. 216f., and the Growing Leaders course, session 6.

2 R. Bauckham, *Gospel Women* (London/New York: T & T Clark, 2002), p. 110.

3 Bauckham, *Gospel Women*, p. 111.

4 Bauckham, *Gospel Women*, p. 193.

5 R. Edwards, *The Case for Women's Ministry* (London: SPCK, 1989), p. 51, citing Raymond Brown.

6 T. K. Seim, *The Double Message: Patterns of Gender in Luke–Acts* (London/New York: T & T Clark, 1994), p. 96.

7 Edwards, *Women's Ministry*, p. 44.

8 Chrysostom refers to her as an apostle in his *Epistle to the Romans*, 3I.

9 K. L. King, 'Prophetic Power and Women's Authority: The Case of the Gospel of Mary', in *Women Priests and Prophets through Two Millennia of Christianity*, ed. B. M. Kienzle and P. J. Walker (Berkeley: University of California Press, 1998), p. 27.

10 C. C. James, *Lost Women of the Bible* (Michigan: Zondervan, 2005), p. 199.

11 Initially leadership roles appear to have been fluid, but in the first couple of centuries the threefold order of ministry began to emerge, and

there is evidence that initially women were ordained as deacons and presbyters, at least in some parts of the Church. The *Acts of Philip* and the *Martyrdom of Matthew* do not argue for female presbyters but assume their existence. But from the second half of the fourth century the ordination of women was systematically opposed: there are a number of places in early church documents where women are barred from certain roles (which also assumes their existence); for example, the Council of Laodicea (AD 364) and the church father Epiphanius (fourth century) condemned the establishment of female presbyters.

Why was women's leadership restricted? For a variety of reasons, it seems: women's supposed inferiority (church fathers thought women 'untrustworthy and of mediocre intelligence', 'easily carried away and light-minded', and Tertullian believed that women were 'not the image of God'); women's supposed guilt – writers linked women with the Fall and Eve: 'the woman taught once and ruined all'; and women's supposed impurity: with the rise of sacramentalism, women were progressively excluded from the sacred because of fear of contamination associated with the blood of menstruation and childbirth.

3 'More Spirited than Lions'

1 This title is relatively frequently used of Mary Magdalene by medieval authors, including Peter Abelard [PL 178, col. 845]. It appears to be derived from the description of her by Hippolytus in his Commentary on the Song of Songs.

2 See U. Eisen, *Women Officeholders in Early Christianity: Epigraphical and Literary Studies* (Collegeville, MN: Liturgical Press, 2000), pp. 50–2. The Byzantine liturgy honours Junia as an apostle, and Mary Magdalene and Thecla as 'equal to the apostles' (Eisen, *Women Officeholders*, p. 48). For Mary Magdalene as an apostle, see also A. G. Brock, *Mary Magdalene* (Cambridge, MA: Harvard University Press, 2002) and S. Petersen, *'Zerstört die Werke der Weiblichkeit!': Maria Magdalena, Salome und andere Jüngerinnen Jesu in christlich-gnostischen Schriften* (Leiden: Brill, 1999).

3 There has been much recent discussion about the gender of Junia and the description of her as an apostle: see, for instance, E. J. Epp, *Junia: The First Woman Apostle* (Minneapolis, MN: Fortress Press, 2005), who summarizes the literature. Compare also J. A. Fitzmyer, *Romans: A New Translation with Introduction and Commentary* (New York/London: Doubleday, 1993), pp. 738–9; J. Thorley, 'Junia, a Woman Apostle,' in *Novum Testamentum*, 38 (1996), pp. 18–29; L. L. Belleville, 'Ιουνιαν · · · εθπι/σημθι εθν τοι=φ αθποτ/λοιφ: A Re-examination of Romans 16.7 in

Light of Primary Source Materials', in *New Testament Studies*, 51 (2005), pp. 231–49. All these authors take Junia to be an outstanding apostle; a counter-argument is offered by M. H. Burer and D. B. Wallace, 'Was Junia Really an Apostle?' in *New Testament Studies*, 47 (2000), pp. 76–91.

4 John Chrysostom, *Hom. Ep. Paul. ad Rom.*, p. 31.

5 John Calvin, *Commentarius in epistolam Pauli ad Romanos* (1556), ed. T. H. L. Parker (Leiden: Brill, 1981), p. 324.

6 Chrysostom, *Hom. Ep. Paul. ad Rom.*, p. 31.

7 A. Jensen, *Thekla, die Apostolin: ein apokrypher Text neu entdeckt* (Gütersloh: Chr. Kaiser, 1999). See also Eisen, *Women Officeholders*, pp. 51–2.

8 For Nino's life, see *The Dictionary of Georgian National Biography* (http://www.georgianbiography.com/bios/n/nino/htm [accessed 17 December 2009]). For accounts of her as an apostle, compare Eisen, *Women Officeholders*, pp. 53–4.

9 Tertullian, *De bapt.*, 17.

10 *Did. Ap.*, ch. 15; *Didascalia Apostolorum*, tr. R. H. Connolly (Oxford: Clarendon Press, 1929), p. 132.

11 Epp, *Junia*, p. 34. For interpretations of Prisca, see D. A. Kurek-Chomycz, 'Is There an "Anti-Priscan" Tendency in the Manuscripts? Some Textual Problems with Prisca and Aquila', in *Journal for Biblical Literature*, 125 (2006), pp. 107–28.

12 Hildegard of Bingen, *Scivias*, part I, vision 1; compare Hildegard of Bingen, *Scivias*, tr. B. Hozeski (Santa Fe, NM: Bear & Company, 1986), p. 7.

13 Hildegard of Bingen, *Scivias*, prologue, tr. B. Hozeski, p. 1.

14 *The Letters of Hildegard of Bingen*, tr. J. L. Baird and R. K. Ehrmann (Oxford: OUP, 1994), vol. 1, p. 53.

15 Mechthild of Magdeburg, *The Flowing Light of the Godhead*, tr. F. Tobin (New York: Paulist Press, 1998), p. 59.

16 Mechthild, *Flowing Light*, p. 61.

17 Mechthild, *Flowing Light*, pp. 96–7.

18 Mechthild, *Flowing Light*, p. 292.

19 Margaret Porette, *The Mirror of Simple Souls*, tr. E. Colledge, J. C. Marler and J. Grant (Notre Dame: University of Notre Dame Press, 1999), ch. 96, p. 120.

20 For Marguerite Porète, see A. Passenier, 'Der Lustgarten des Leibes und die Freiheit der Seele: Wege der Mittelalterlichen Frauenspiritualität', in E. Hartlieb and C. Methuen, eds. *Sources and Resources of Feminist Theologies* (Kampen: Kok Pharos, 1997), pp. 192–216; Bernard McGinn, *The Flowering of Mysticism: Men and Women in the New Mysticism (1200–1350)* (New York: Crossroad, 1998).

21 Julian of Norwich, *Revelations of Divine Love*, tr. J. B. Holloway, from the British Library Manuscript Sloane 2499, collated with the Westminster Cathedral Manuscript, the Paris Bibliothèque Nationale Anglais 40 Manuscript, and the British Library Amherst Manuscript (http://www.umilta.net/elovepref.html [accessed 8 September 2009]), First Revelation, Ch. 9.

22 Julian of Norwich, *Revelations*, First Revelation, Ch. 9.

23 Julian of Norwich, *Revelations*, First Revelation, Ch. 9.

24 P. Matheson, *Argula von Grumbach: A Woman's Voice in the Reformation* (Edinburgh: T & T Clark, 1995), p. 176, referring to Joel 2.

25 Matheson, *Argula von Grumbach*, pp. 177–8, referring to 1 Cor. 2.

26 Matheson, *Argula von Grumbach*, pp. 176–7, referring to John 7.

27 Matheson, *Argula von Grumbach*, pp. 177, referring to Luke 5.

28 Matheson, *Argula von Grumbach*, p. 180, referring to Mark, last chapter.

29 Matheson, *Argula von Grumbach*, pp. 183–4.

30 Matheson, *Argula von Grumbach*, p. 185, referring to Judge 4.

31 Matheson, *Argula von Grumbach*, pp. 185–95, referring to Judge 4.

32 Matheson, *Argula von Grumbach*, pp. 182–3, referring to Numbers 22.

33 For the life of Katharina Schütz Zell, see E. A. McKee, *Katharina Schütz Zell, Vol. 1: The Life and Work of a Sixteenth-century Reformer* (Leiden: Brill, 1999); selected English translations in Katharina Schütz Zell, *Church Mother: The Writings of a Protestant Reformer in Sixteenth-century Germany*, ed. and tr. E. McKee (Chicago/London: University of Chicago Press, 2006).

4 Some Reflections on Women and Leadership

1 P. E. Anson, *The Call of the Cloister: Religious Communities and Kindred Bodies in the Anglican Communion* (London: SPCK, 1955).

2 Advisory Council on the Relations of Bishops and Religious Communities, *A Handbook of the Religious Life* (Norwich: Canterbury Press, 5th edition, 2004).

3 C. W. Bynum, *Fragmentation and Redemption: Essays on Gender and the Body in Medieval Religion* (New York: Zone Books, 1992).

5 Reflections on Women, Authority and the Church

1 In general, in the Episcopal Church bishops do not appoint priests, except perhaps to mission churches or to troubled parishes upon request.

The normal process is that a search committee, organized by the parish, vets candidates and then presents a slate of two or three candidates to the vestry for interviewing and then election. The bishop must approve the final selection.

2 I am aware that in describing the maleness and femaleness of human beings the grammatically correct term is sex, not gender, but 'sex' has become so charged a word in our culture that using it correctly becomes distracting. I have therefore for the most part used the incorrect but more acceptable term 'gender'.

3 Vestries were historically conditioned to think of priests as male, many having never even seen a female priest before the search process. So without ever intending to discriminate and without much awareness of the strength of that conditioning, parishes would often call less qualified men over more qualified women, no matter how well the interviews went.

4 After I left, the mission congregation engaged in a search and called a vicar who over the course of the next two years took membership to 200.

5 Notable exceptions were the three dioceses in which women's ordination was (out of 111) not recognized until 2009.

6 It is only when I step out of the context of the Episcopal Church into the Anglican Communion that I feel marked by my gender once again.

7 In TEC, parishes elect their own rector or priest-in-charge, but the rector or priest-in-charge hires clergy staff without canonical requirement for permission of vestry, congregation or bishop for that matter, although for assistants called from other dioceses, the bishop must approve through the granting of a Licence-to-officiate.

8 For interesting statistics on deployment, compensation and gender in the Episcopal Church, go to www.cpg.org and click on 'Research'. Even the latest figures recorded, from 2007, show the gender discrepancy. In particular, note Matthew Price's report for 2007, pp. 2, 3 and 5.

9 D. Tannen, *Talking from 9 to 5* (New York: William Morrow, 1994).

10 Tannen, *Talking from 9 to 5*, p. 161.

11 Tannen, *Talking from 9 to 5*, p. 162.

12 Tannen, *Talking from 9 to 5*, p. 167.

13 Tannen, *Talking from 9 to 5*, pp. 107–10.

14 A priest friend of mine has suggested that in blessing we use 'In the name of the Father and the Son, and the Holy Spirit: the Mother of us all.' The difficulty is that when spoken, this formulation makes it sound as if what is meant is that the Holy Spirit is the Mother of us all,

which misses the point entirely. What my friend means is that the Holy Trinity in its entirety is the Mother of us all, as the matrix of our being. Conceptually, I think he is on to something.

7 Size Matters

1 To put this in a wider context, it must be appreciated that within the 16,000 churches nationally the average electoral roll figure is about 50 and as an overview a large church, excluding the very large churches of over 500 or so, would have approximately 150–200 electoral roll. The large church definition was given in a short telephone interview with the National Officer for Statistics, the Revd Lynda Barley, who has an overview of the national statistics. This is not proven but as a general picture is useful. This also puts in perspective that Rochester diocese has many larger churches within its boundaries. Figures come from diocesan handbooks.

2 R. Ward, 'Women Clergy and Deployment', CPAS article online at: http://www.cpas.org.uk/womeninleadership/content/women_in_leadership_530.php?e=720.

3 R. Ward, 'Women Clergy and Deployment'.

4 P. Jamieson, *Living at the Edge: Sacrament and Solidarity in Leadership* (London: Mowbray, 1997), p. 139. She offers this in a discussion on authority for leadership, flagging up that although men find it easier to assume authority in the first place, they can find it harder at times to move to a more mutual and relational form of authority later on.

5 Ward, 'Women Clergy and Deployment'.

6 Office for National Statistics, 26 September 2008, 'More Women in Work but Half in Part-Time Jobs', online at: http://www.statistics.gov.uk/pdfdir/fng0908.pdf.

7 C. Rees, ed., *Voices of This Calling: Experiences of the First Generation of Women Priests* (Norwich: Canterbury Press, 2002).

8 Rees, *Voices of This Calling*, pp. 111–13, 115–17, 118–21, 124–5, 126–7.

9 Figures here are based on research using figures from the 2008 Rochester diocesan handbook.

10 There may be benefices with combined electoral rolls that add up to this number.

11 R. Ward, *Growing Women Leaders: Nurturing Women's Leadership in the Church* (Abingdon: CPAS/BRF, 2008), see chapter 7, p. 157: 'It has been shown in a variety of contexts that many men overestimate their abilities and many women underestimate them.'

12 Of the ten largest churches in Rochester diocese at least six have an evangelical theological tendency.

13 A. Watson, 'The Recruitment and Deployment of Women Clergy in the Larger Church' The Second National Larger Anglican Churches Conference: 20 November 2007. (CPAS source, received March 2009).

14 Watson, 'Recruitment and Deployment of Women Clergy'. Watson refers to 'homebuilders' who benefit from toddler groups and daytime activities.

15 Watson, 'Recruitment and Deployment of Women Clergy'.

16 Ward, *Growing Women Leaders*, p. 189.

17 General overview of national statistics given by Lynda Barley, Church House, London.

18 B. Jackson, *The Road to Growth: Towards a Thriving Church* (London: Church House Publishing, 2005), p. 44.

19 This is borne out in the short survey of women incumbents in this diocese. The sample, however, is very small and therefore could be less than representative.

20 E. Armstrong, 'My Glass Ceiling is Self-Imposed', *Globe and Mail Update*, 15 December 2004 at 8:27 a.m., http://www.theglobeandmail.com/servlet/story/RTGAM.20041215.gtfacts15/BNStory/einsider/?query=women.

21 Armstrong, 'My Glass Ceiling is Self-Imposed'.

22 C. Becker, *Leading Women: How Church Women can Avoid Leadership Traps and Negotiate the Gender Maze* (Nashville: Abingdon Press, 1996), p. 57 quotes Swartz who puts this forward in relation to the business world and the different expectations that are held by men in management about women, but not for men.

23 J. Porter, *Leading Ladies: Transformative Biblical Images for Women's Leadership* (Philadelphia: Innis Free Press, 2000), pp. 13–16.

24 D. T. Alexander and D. W. Baker, eds, *Dictionary of the Old Testament Pentateuch* (Leicester: IVP, 2003), pp. 897–903.

25 J. Porter, *Leading Ladies*, drawn and concluded from Porter's work.

26 Luke 10.38–42.

27 Ward, *Growing Women Leaders*, p. 127.

28 While acknowledging that the sample is small and only from women.

29 1 Corinthians 12.

30 Survey quotes.

31 Survey quotes.

32 Becker, *Leading Women*, p. 58.

33 *Church Times*, 17 October 2008.

34 Reading profiles of advertised vacancies from the *Church of England Newspaper* and in the *Church Times* bears this out.

35 This will, one hopes, be true of any priest regardless of gender.

8 Women and Leadership

1 I am grateful to both Sara Miles and June Osborne for reading a draft of this essay and discussing the nature of leadership in the Church with me. Portions of the first section of this essay first appeared in *Third Way*.

2 J. Woodward, 'Richard: The Person and the Bishop', in M. Brierley, ed., *Public Life and the Place of the Church: Reflections to Honour the Bishop of Oxford* (Aldershot: Ashgate, 2006), p. 22.

3 http://www.episcopalchurch.org/3577_82917_ENG_HTM.htm.

4 B. Harris, 'Living the Change: On Being the First Woman Bishop in the Anglican Communion', in H. Harris and J. Shaw, eds, *The Call for Women Bishops* (London: SPCK, 2004), p. 29.

5 Quoted by Henry Mayr-Harting in his address at Chadwick's memorial service in Christ Church Cathedral, Oxford, 27 September 2008. See: http://www.chch.ox.ac.uk/images/stories/News/downloads/chadwickhmh.pdf.

6 See R. Lyman, 'Women Bishops in Antiquity: Apostolicity and Ministry', in Harris and Shaw, *Call for Women Bishops*.

7 Alison Webster discusses the notion of the gift in theological terms in *You are Mine: Reflections on Who we Are* (London: SPCK, 2009).

8 See O. Brafman and R. A. Beckstrom, *The Starfish and the Spider: The Unstoppable Power of Leaderless Organizations* (New York: Penguin, 2006).

9 Benedict Revisited

1 Rule of St Benedict, Prologue.

2 Benedict makes provision for people with different needs (Chapters 34, 39 and 40) and has last-resort guidance on what to do when monastics hit each other (Chapter 70), which suggests that common commitment at times was hard to maintain.

3 In Chapter 71 he reminds us that 'obedience is of such value that it should be shown not only to the superior but all members of the community should be obedient to each other in the sure knowledge that this way of obedience is the one that will take them straight to God.'

4 For example, he addresses the question of how to respond to orders that seem impossible and not acting as advocate for another (Rule of St Benedict, Chapters 68 and 69), which might be worth exploring for any insights for us in a different context.

5 M. Casey, *Strangers to the City* (Brewster, MA: Paraclete Press, 2005), p. 191.

6 Hebrews 5.8.

7 Rule of St Benedict, Chapter 3.

8 A few adjustments were made; for example, the midnight service of Matins disappeared.

9 G. Moorhouse, *The Last Office: 1539 and the Dissolution of a Monastery* (London: Weidenfeld and Nicolson, 2008). Moorhouse notes that the evidence that remains is of a collective rather than individual nature, p. 207.

10 Moorhouse, *Last Office*, p. 205.

11 See, for example, W. Brueggemann, *The Psalms and the Life of Faith* (Minneapolis: Fortress Press, 1995), pp. 8ff., where he applies Paul Ricoeur's insights to psalmody.

12 Information about the cathedral's Benedictine weekends and days can be found on the cathedral's website.

13 Hebrews 11.1.

14 R. Bolt, *A Man for All Seasons* (Oxford: Heinemann, 1960), Act 2.

15 The famous pitfall is a conversation between unwary British and Americans about tabling a document and then having it slated. The gulf of understanding is enormous.

16 J. Chittister, *The Rule of Benedict: Insight for the Ages* (New York: Crossroad, 1996), pp. 140–1.

17 John 1.39.

18 Rule of St Benedict, Chapter 4.

10 In Search of a Spirituality of Authority

1 A. de Saint-Exupéry, *The Little Prince*; tr. K. Woods (London: Pan Books, 1974).

2 Saint-Exupéry, *Little Prince*, p. 70.

3 Saint-Exupéry, *Little Prince*, p. 9.

11 'For God's Sake'

1 See further J. Tetley, 'The Use of the Bible in Ecumenical Dialogue involving Anglicans', in P. Avis, ed., *Paths to Unity: Explorations*

in Ecumenical Method (London: Church House Publishing, 2004), pp. 52–5.

2 R. Bauckham, *Jesus and the God of Israel: God Crucified and Other Essays on the New Testament's Christology of Divine Identity* (Milton Keynes: Paternoster, 2008), p. 237.

3 Bauckham, *Jesus and the God of Israel*, p. 251.

4 P. Ellingworth, *The Epistle to the Hebrews: A Commentary on the Greek Text* (Michigan: Eerdmans/Milton Keynes: Paternoster, 1993), p. 373.

12 Evangelical Women, Spirituality and Leadership

1 M. Guenther, *Holy Listening: The Art of Spiritual Direction* (London: DLT, 1992).

2 David Bebbington, in *Evangelicalism in Modern Britain: A History from the 1730s to the 1980s* (London: Unwin Hyman, 1989), pointed to a fourth key feature, that of conversionism; see below.

3 I am indebted to Pauline Warner, *Women's Icons of Ministry* (Nottingham: Grove, 1994) for drawing my attention to Joseph. I have never heard a sermon about him.

4 This relates to the vexed question of the so-called feminization of the Church, which I have no space to deal with here. Suffice it to say that if men and women are allowed to be themselves, then men can be men whether they are logical and directive or intuitive and gentle, and the same applies to women.

5 See Acts 17 and the Gospels, *passim*.

13 What Clergy Do, Especially When it Looks Like Nothing

1 N. Stadlen, *What Mothers Do: Especially When it Looks Like Nothing* (London: Piatkus, 2004).

2 Stadlen, *What Mothers Do*, p. 18.

3 Stadlen, *What Mothers Do*, p. 24.

4 A. Russell, *The Clerical Profession* (London: SPCK, 1980); M. Percy, *Clergy: The Origin of Species* (London: Continuum, 2006).

5 U. T. Holmes, *The Future Shape of Ministry: A Theological Projection* (New York: Seabury, 1971), p. 245.

6 R. Towler and A. P. M. Coxon, *The Fate of the Anglican Clergy: A Sociological Study* (London: Macmillan, 1979), p. 54. This study followed students from theological college, through analysis of their

future careers and questionnaires informed by the work of Eysenck and the Allport-Vernon-Lindsey study of Values.

7 Stadlen, *What Mothers Do*, p. 257.

15 Episcope and Eiscope

1 M. C. Beaton, *Agatha Raisin and the Case of the Curious Curate* (New York: St Martin's Press, 2003), p. 97.

2 See S. Hauerwas, *Character and the Christian Life: A Study in Theological Ethics* (Texas: Trinity University Press, 1974); S. Hauerwas, *A Community of Character: Toward a Constructive Christian Social Ethic* (Notre Dame: University of Notre Dame Press, 1981).

3 *Book of Common Prayer* (Cambridge: Cambridge University Press, 2007), p. 594.

4 See, for example, *Henry IV Pt II*, Act V scene i: 'It is certain that ignorant carriage is caught, as men take diseases, of one another; therefore let men take heed of their company.'

5 *Common Worship: Services and Prayers for the Church of England: Ordination Services Study Edition* (London: Church House Publishing, 2007), p. 61.

6 *Common Worship*, p. 32.

7 All biblical quotations are from the New Revised Standard Version (NRSV) unless indicated otherwise.

8 See F. W. Danker, *A Greek-English Lexicon of the New Testament and Other Early Christian Literature* (BDAG, 2000), p. 379.

9 E. T. Charry, *By the Renewing of Your Minds: The Pastoral Function of Christian Doctrine* (New York/Oxford: Oxford University Press, 1997), p. 76. For the neologism 'aretegenic', that is to say, conducive to virtue, *areté*, see p. 19.

10 See Revelation 7.17, Hebrews 13.10 and John 10.11–14.

11 See D. J. Harrington, ed., *Sacra Pagina: I Peter, Jude and 2 Peter* (Collegeville, MN: Liturgical Press, 2003), p. 80.

12 So it would appear from, for example, 1 Corinthians 6.

13 C. S. Lewis, *The Screwtape Letters* (London: HarperCollins, 1998), p. 9.

14 Hauerwas, *A Community of Character*.

15 Gregory the Great, *The Book of Pastoral Rule*, tr. J. Barmby (Edinburgh: T & T Clark/Michigan: Eerdmans, 1997).

16 R. Gula, *Ethics in Pastoral Ministry* (Mahwah, NJ: Paulist Press, 1996), p. 32; J. Soskice, *The Kindness of God: Metaphor, Gender, and Religious Language* (Oxford: Oxford University Press, 2007), pp. 22, 25.

17 Gula, *Ethics in Pastoral Ministry*, p. 33.

16 The Evangelical Burden and Imperative

1 This is a strange word to us in reference to the women, but I believe it is justified as there has been within the debate a right concern to 'protect' them from being placed within a position that compromised them within the House of Bishops, within their dioceses or more particularly as they sought to engage pastorally and appropriately with those who found their existence difficult.

2 Barth, *Church Dogmatics*, IV/1, p. 724, quoted in J. B. Webster, *Word and Church: Essays in Christian Dogmatics* (Edinburgh: T & T Clark, 2001), p. 208.

3 Something similar (though not identical) to this was established in Melbourne as a result of the *Paul Report for the Diocese of Melbourne* in 1964. 'The report gave birth to the aphorism "the college of bishops is the bishop of the diocese". It felt that there were important precedents for the principle (which it was prepared to trace back to Cyprian, Bishop of Carthage, 248–58)' (L. A. Paul, *A Church by Daylight: A Reappraisement of the Church of England and its Future*, London: Macmillan, 1973, chapter 4, The Episcopacy, p. 144).

In many ways it is what Oxford diocese moved towards under Richard Harries, with its model of area bishops, each with their own area responsibilities and then particular responsibility within the senior staff.

4 When the Rochester Report, *Women Bishops in the Church of England*, was published in 2004 there were many women who reacted negatively to Annex 3, 'What Does a Bishop Do?' I have lost track of the number of conversations I had at that time (and indeed I continue to have) with women clergy who said that it was clearly a job for workaholics and one that did not allow space for the needs of a family or of the individual; that it gave little room for creative development and response to the pastoral needs of the people.

5 It is common among doctors and university lecturers, for example, for responsibility for chairing to rotate among a group of colleagues.

6 Transfiguring Episcope Conference, Cuddesdon, July 2008.

7 Using Peter Brierley's definition of a large church (over 350), there are only two women leading such churches – contrast two female deans in the 42 cathedrals. Peter Brierley, formerly Director of Christian Research and MARC Europe, alongside John Dunnett of CPAS, facilitates the National Larger Anglican Church Conferences, for which a larger church is defined as being over 350.

8 AWESOME – Anglican Women Evangelicals, Supporting our Ordained Ministry – a group formed after NEAC4 (National Evangelical Anglican Congress in 2003) to raise the profile of and provide support, equipping and ongoing training for evangelical women within the Church of England.

BIBLIOGRAPHY

Advisory Council on the Relations of Bishops and Religious Communities, *A Handbook of the Religious Life* (Norwich: Canterbury Press,
5th edition, 2004).

Alexander, D. T. and Baker, D. W., eds, *Dictionary of the Old Testament Pentateuch* (Leicester: IVP, 2003).

Amos, C., 'A Staging Post on the Journey: Transfiguration and the Anglican Way', *Anglican World*; Trinity 2007, available at: http://www.
anglicancommunion.org/resources/aw/downloads/126/aw126b.pdf.

Anson, P. E., *The Call of the Cloister: Religious Communities and Kindred Bodies in the Anglican Communion* (London: SPCK, 1955).

Armstrong, E., 'My Glass Ceiling is Self-Imposed', *Globe and Mail
Update* 15 December 2004 at 8.27 A.M., online at: http://www.
theglobeandmail.com/servlet/story/RTGAM.20041215.gtfacts15/
BNStory/einsider/?query=women.

Avis, P., ed., *Paths to Unity: Explorations in Ecumenical Method* (London: Church House Publishing, 2004).

Bebbington, D., *Evangelicalism in Modern Britain: A History from the
1730s to the 1980s* (London: Unwin Hyman, 1989).

Bauckham, R., *Gospel Women* (London/New York: T & T Clark,
2002).

Bauckham, R., *Jesus and the God of Israel: God Crucified and Other
Essays on the New Testament's Christology of Divine Identity* (Milton Keynes: Paternoster, 2008).

Beaton, M. C., *Agatha Raisin and the Case of the Curious Curate* (New
York: St Martin's Press, 2003).

Becker, C., *Leading Women: How Church Women can Avoid Leadership Traps and Negotiate the Gender Maze* (Nashville: Abingdon
Press, 1996).

Belleville, 'Ὀϊουνιαν ... εϋπι/σημοι εϋν τοι=φ αϋποστο/λοιφ: a re-examination of Romans 16.7 in light of primary source materials', in *New
Testament Studies*, 51 (2005).

Bolt, R., *A Man for All Seasons* (Oxford: Heinemann, 1960).

Brafman, O. and Beckstrom, R. A., *The Starfish and the Spider: The Unstoppable Power of Leaderless Organizations* (New York: Penguin, 2006).

Brierley, M., ed., *Public Life and the Place of the Church: Reflections to Honour the Bishop of Oxford* (Aldershot: Ashgate, 2006).

Brock, A. G., *Mary Magdalene, The First Apostle: The Struggle for Authority* (Cambridge, MA: Harvard Divinity School, 1999).

Brueggemann, W., 'Trajectories in Old Testament Literature and the Sociology of Ancient Israel', JBL, 98, 1979.

Brueggemann, W., *The Psalms and the Life of Faith* (Minneapolis: Augsburg Fortress Press, 1995).

Burer, M. H. and Wallace, D. B., 'Was Junia Really an Apostle?', *New Testament Studies*, 47 (2000).

Bynum, C. W., *Fragmentation and Redemption: Essays on Gender and the Body in Medieval Religion* (New York: Zone Books, 1992).

Casey, M., *Strangers to the City* (Brewster, MA: Paraclete Press, 2005).

Charry, E. T., *By the Renewing of Your Minds: The Pastoral Function of Christian Doctrine* (New York/Oxford: Oxford University Press, 1997).

Chittister, J., *The Rule of St Benedict: Insight for the Ages* (New York: Crossroad, 1996).

Church of England, *Book of Common Prayer* (Cambridge: Cambridge University Press, 2007).

Church of England, *Common Worship: Services and Prayers for the Church of England* (London: Church House Publishing, 2007).

Church of England Signposts Statement, online at: http://www.anglicancommunion.org/ministry/theological/signposts/english.cfm.

Calvin, J., *Commentarius in epistolam Pauli ad Romanos* (1556) ed. T. H. L. Parker, Studies in Christian Thought 22 (Leiden: Brill, 1981).

Connolly, R. H., tr., *Didascalia Apostolorum* (Oxford: Clarendon Press, 1929).

Danker, F. W., *A Greek-English Lexicon of the New Testament and Other Early Christian Literature* (BDAG, 2000).

Edwards, R. B., *The Case for Women's Ministry* (London: SPCK, 1989).

Eisen, U., *Women Officeholders in Early Christianity: Epigraphical and Literary Studies* (Collegeville, MN: Liturgical Press, 2000).

Ellingworth, P., *The Epistle to the Hebrews: A Commentary on the Greek Text* (Michigan: Eerdmans/Milton Keynes: Paternoster, 1993).

Epp, E. J., *Junia: The First Woman Apostle* (Minneapolis: Fortress Press).

Fitzmyer, J. A., *Romans: A New Translation with Introduction and Commentary* (New York/London: Doubleday, 1993).

Gaventa, B. R., *Our Mother Saint Paul* (Louiseville, KY: Westminster John Knox, 2007).

Guenther, M., *Holy Listening: The Art of Spiritual Direction* (London: DLT, 1992).

Gula, R., *Ethics in Pastoral Ministry* (Mahwah, NJ: Paulist Press, 1996).

Harrington, D. J., ed., *Sacra Pagina: 1 Peter, Jude and 2 Peter* (Collegeville, MN: Liturgical Press, 2003).

Harris, B., 'Living the Change: On Being the First Woman Bishop in the Anglican Communion', in H. Harris and J. Shaw, eds, *The Call for Women Bishops* (London: SPCK, 2004).

Harris, H. and Shaw, J., eds, *The Call for Women Bishops* (London: SPCK, 2004).

Hartlieb, E. and Methuen, C., eds., *Sources and Resources of Feminist Theologies*, Yearbook of the European Society of Women in Theological Research 5 (Kampen: Kok Pharos, 1997).

Hauerwas, S., *Character and the Christian Life: A Study in Theological Ethics* (Texas: Trinity University Press, 1974).

Hildegard of Bingen, *The Letters of Hildegard of Bingen*, tr. J. L. Baird and R. K. Ehrmann (Oxford: Oxford University Press, 1994).

Hildegard of Bingen, *Hildegard of Bingen's Scivias*, tr. B. Hozeski (Santa Fe, NM: Bear & Company, 1986).

Holmes, U. T., *The Future Shape of Ministry: A Theological Projection* (New York: Seabury Press, 1971).

Jackson, B., *The Road to Growth: Towards a Thriving Church* (London: Church House Publishing, 2005).

James, C. C., *Lost Women of the Bible* (Michigan: Zondervan, 2005).

Jamieson, P., *Living at the Edge: Sacrament and Solidarity in Leadership* (London: Mowbray, 1997).

Jensen, A., *Thekla die Apostolin: ein apokrypher Text neu entdeckt* (Gütersloh: Chr. Kaiser, 1999).

Julian of Norwich, *Revelations of Divine Love*, tr. J. B. Holloway, British Library Manuscript Sloane 2499 collated with the Westminster Cathedral Manuscript, the Paris, Bibliothèque Nationale, Anglais 40 Manuscript, and the British Library Amherst Manuscript, online at: http://www.umilta.net/elovepref.html (accessed 8 September 2009).

Kienzle, B. M. and Walker, P. J., *Women Preachers and Prophets through Two Millennia of Christianity* (Berkeley: University of California Press, 1998).

King, K. L., 'Prophetic Power and Women's Authority: The Case of the Gospel of Mary', in *Women Priests and Prophets through Two*

Millennia of Christianity, B. M. Kienzle and P. J. Walker, eds, (Berkeley: University of California Press, 1998).

King, N. SJ, *The New Testament Freshly Translated* (Stowmarket: Kevin Mayhew, 2004).

Kroeger, C. C. and Evans, M. J., eds, *IVP Women's Bible Commentary* (Downers Grove: Intervarsity Press, 2002).

Kurek-Chomycz, D. A., 'Is There an "Anti-Priscian" Tendency in the Manuscripts? Some Textual Problems with Prisca and Aquila', *Journal for Biblical Literature*, 125 (2006).

Lawrence, J., *Growing Leaders* (BRF/CPAS, 2004).

Lewis, C. S., *The Screwtape Letters* (London: HarperCollins, 1998).

Lyman, R., 'Women Bishops in Antiquity: Apostolicity and Ministry', in H. Harris and J. Shaw, eds, *The Call for Women Bishops* (London: SPCK, 2004).

Madigan, K. and Osiek, C., eds, *Ordained Women in the Early Church: A Documentary History* (Baltimore: Johns Hopkins University Press, 2005).

Matheson, P., *Argula von Grumbach: A Woman's Voice in the Reformation* (Edinburgh: T & T Clark, 1995).

McGinn, B., *The Flowering of Mysticism: Men and Women in the New Mysticism (1200–1350)*, The Presence of God, vol. 3 (New York: Crossroad, 1998).

McKee, E. A., *Katharina Schütz Zell: The Life and Work of a Sixteenth-century Reformer* (Leiden: Brill, 1999).

Mechthild of Magdeburg, *The Flowing Light of the Godhead*, tr. F. Tobin, Classics of Western Spirituality (New York: Paulist Press, 1998).

Miller, S., *Women in Mark's Gospel* (Edinburgh: T & T Clark, 2004).

Moorhouse, G., *The Last Office: 1539 and the Dissolution of a Monastery* (London: Weidenfeld and Nicolson, 2008).

Office for National Statistics, 'More Women in Work but Half in Part-Time Jobs', online at: http://www.statistics.gov.uk/pdfdir/fng0908.pdf.

Passenier, A., 'Der Lustgarten des Leibes und die Freiheit der Seele: Wege der Mittelalterlichen Frauenspiritualität', in E. Hartlieb and C. Methuen, eds, *Sources and Resources of Feminist Theologies*, Yearbook of the European Society of Women in Theological Research 5; (Kampen: Kok Pharos, 1997).

Percy, M., *Clergy: The Origin of Species* (London: Continuum, 2006).

Peterson, S., *'Zerstört die Werke der Weiblichkeit!': Mary Magdalena, Salome und andere Jüngerinnen Jesu in christlich-gnostischen Schriften* (Leiden: Brill, 1999).

Pierce, R. W. and Groothuis, R. M., eds, *Discovering Biblical Equality* (Nottingham: IVP, 2005).

Porette, M., *The Mirror of Simple Souls*, tr. E. Colledge, J. C. Marler and J. Grant, Notre Dame texts in Medieval Culture 6 (Notre Dame: University of Notre Dame Press, 1999).

Porter, J., *Leading Ladies: Transformative Biblical Images for Women's Leadership* (Philadelphia: Innis Free Press, 2000).

Ramsey, M., *The Glory of God and the Transfiguration of Christ* (London: DLT, 1949/1967).

Rees, C., ed., *Voices of This Calling: Experiences of the First Generation of Women Priests* (Norwich: Canterbury Press, 2002).

Russell, A., *The Clerical Profession* (London: Piatkus, 2004).

Saint-Exupéry, A., *The Little Prince*, tr. K. Woods (London: Pan Books, 1974).

Seim, T. K., *The Double Message: Patterns of Gender in Luke–Acts* (London/New York: T & T Clark, 1994).

Solskice, J., *The Kindness of God: Metaphor, Gender, and Religious Language* (Oxford: Oxford University Press, 2007).

Spencer, A. B., 'Jesus' Treatment of Women in the Gospels', in R. W. Pierce and R. M. Groothuis, eds, *Discovering Biblical Equality* (Nottingham: IVP, 2005).

Stadlen, N., *What Mothers Do: Especially When it Looks Like Nothing* (London: Piatkus, 2004).

Tannen, D., *Talking from 9 to 5* (New York: William Morrow, 1994).

Tetley, J., 'The Use of the Bible in Ecumenical Dialogue Involving Anglicans', in P. Avis, ed., *Paths to Unity: Explorations in Ecumenical Method* (London: Church House Publishing, 2004).

The Dictionary of Georgian National Biography, online at: http://www.georgianbiography.com/bios/n/nino/htm (accessed 17 December 2009).

Thorley, J., 'Junia, a Woman Apostle', in *Novum Testamentum*, 38 (1996).

Towler, R. and Coxon, A. P. M., *The Fate of Anglican Clergy: A Sociological Study* (London: Macmillan, 1979).

Ward, B., tr., *The Prayers and Meditations of Saint Anselm* (Harmondsworth/New York: Penguin, 1973).

Ward, R., *Growing Women Leaders* (BRF/CPAS, 2008).

Ward, R., 'Women Clergy and Deployment', CPAS article online at: http://www.cpas.org.uk/womeninleadership/content/women_in_leadership_530.php?e=720.

Warner, P., *Women's Icons of Ministry*, Grove Pastoral Series, 60 (Nottingham: Grove, 1994).

Watson, A., 'The Recruitment and Deployment of Women Clergy in the Larger Church', The Second National Larger Anglican Churches

Conference, 20 November 2007 (CPAS source, received March 2009).

Webster, A., *You are Mine: Reflections on Who we Are* (London: SPCK, 2009).

Webster, J. B., *Word and Church: Essays in Christian Dogmatics* (Edinburgh: T & T Clark, 2001).

Woodward, J., 'Richard: The Person and the Bishop', in M. Brierley, ed., *Public Life and the Place of the Church: Reflections to Honour the Bishop of Oxford* (Aldershot: Ashgate, 2006).

Wright, T., 'The Biblical Basis for Women's Service in the Church', paper given in 2004, available on the Fulcrum website, and in *Priscilla Papers*, 20.4, pp. 5–10.

Zell, K. S., *Church Mother: The Writings of a Protestant Reformer in Sixteenth-century Germany*, ed. and tr. E. McKee (Chicago/London: University of Chicago Press, 2006).

INDEX OF NAMES AND SUBJECTS